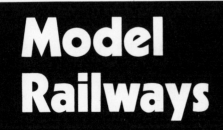

# LOCOMOTIVE
# ALBUM

Edited by
Douglas Doherty

MODEL & ALLIED PUBLICATIONS LTD.

13/35 Bridge Street, Hemel Hempstead, HP1 1EE, Hertfordshire, England

Model and Allied Publications Ltd.
Book Division, Station Road,
Kings Langley, Hertfordshire,
England


© Model & Allied Publications Ltd. 1971
ISBN 0 85242 221 0
First Published 1971
Second Impression 1973

Printed in Great Britain by Page Bros (Norwich) Ltd, Norwich

# CONTENTS

# Prepared at Crewe

## by Lester Crisford

AS a Junior Driver, or Fireman at Crewe, one began his career in a Shunting Link, known as 'The Young Mens Link'. A group of twenty-six young drivers paired with twenty-six young firemen, the Driver would have completed twenty or more years as a Fireman.

The work in this link was varied, but there was very little main line work. The work consisted of shunting freight traffic in the marshalling yard at Basford Hall, shunting passenger and parcel traffic in the station, shunts on various parts of the 'Works' and three weeks preparing, that is to say, getting main line engines ready for the road after they had been serviced, shed slang for this job was 'fatting', a hangover from the days when valve gear was lubricated with tallow. The oil cans used by enginemen were known as tallow pots. It is 'preparing' that I propose to write about here.

On the commencement of a week's preparing, one went to the 'Tool Hut' to select a large tallow pot, an 'N.E.' type was best as these had wide spouts. This, of course, made for quicker oiling and consequently, more meal time. The pot would be hidden away at the end of each shift.

The 'Tool Hut' was, in fact, a lamp room where coal buckets, head lamps, firemen's shovels and coal picks were stored when engines were left on the shed. This hut was a concrete structure situated approximately in the centre of the shed yard.

In the Tool Hut was a character known as the Tool Man, his job was to clean and fill headlamps with paraffin, check fog signals and replace any damaged equipment with new. Tool buckets were hung in rows on the racks provided for the purpose, clean sand being laid under the bucket rack to catch any odd drops of oil, coal picks and shovels were also deposited in racks and the headlamps were put on shelves in pairs.

The Tool Hut at '5A' was spotlessly clean and God help the Fireman who made any mess, he would go down the shed yard with the toolman's "Best Wishes" ringing in his ears (with apologies to 'Bill Wright', retired).

A typical preparing shift would be to book on duty at 10.0 p.m., greet one's mate, and read any

L.M.S. 6100 'Royal Scot' at Crewe in 1939.
*Photo by G. A. Barlow.*

L.M.S. Royal Scot class 4–6–0 6139 'The Welch Regiment' at Crewe. *Photo by G. A. Barlow.*

late notices applicable to oneself. From the Time Office one went down the tunnel to the 'Train Board', this being a very large blackboard on which was marked in chalk every engine at present on the shed, a typical line would be shown thus:-

| Time | Destination | Engine No. | Road | Shed |
|------|-------------|------------|------|------|
| 12.1 | Glasgow | 6110 | 12 | 2 |
| 12.5 | Birmingham | 5332 | 7 | 1 |

'The Board' would best be described as the hub of the shed, as most shed staff and certainly all loco men would have to consult the board before they could begin work. This board is in a permanent position on a wall where one enters No. 1 shed, it is, of course, very well illuminated. To the preparers, the board tells them what sort of a night they are likely to have. Next move is into the Mess-room, where jackets and bags are hung up and the eternal Loco Man's Question is asked, "anybody brewed?".

The set of men would sit in the Mess-room for a few minutes and talk to the other 'sets' while they waited for the 'Outside Foreman' to come and give the work out, a 'set' of men is a Driver and Fireman, there would be three sets preparing.

The Outside Foreman is a former loco man, he is responsible for allocating the engines for various jobs and where necessary, seeing that engines are prepared. The chief 'bogey' is a 'Late Start' and he is naturally going to do his best to see that the motive power dept does not 'buy it'.

The Outside Foreman opens the door and enters the mess-room, he is carrying a writing board under his arm and has a pencil stuck in his trilby, on the writing board are noted all the

engines that are to be prepared. He enquires smilingly if the men are in 'good nick', he then gives the work to the men. The first set are given 6110 (Grenadier Guardsman) to get ready for 12.1 a.m. Glasgow, the second set are given 6201 (Princess Elizabeth) for 1.0 a.m. Glasgow and the third set are told to prepare 5703 (Thunderer) for 1.50 a.m. Barrow. 6201 was a very difficult engine to prepare as underneath were two separate sets of valve gear with a total of 38 oiling points, some of which were extremely difficult to get at, however, once oiled this engine was one of the finest on the road.

The Fireman of the first set would go first to the oil stores for a bundle of cotton waste and look at the 'board' to see where the engine was stabled. The Driver and he would then proceed to the engine. They would go along by the 'Fitters' Square', a large open area of No. 1 Shed, here were to be seen a good collection of giant machine tools for doing heavy repairs on 'stopped' engines. These stopped engines were always marshalled facing the square, this was to facilitate the removal of valves and pistons for cleaning and re-ringing, also it allowed super-heater tubes to be changed. Towards the end of the square was a very old 'Wilson' oil engine, driving a compressor every few minutes, this old timer would burst forth with a really lusty "thump, thump, thump", enough to make one jump out of one's skin.

On No. 12 road No. 1 Shed was a hydraulic hoist, this being used for lifting small engines

Manchester-Euston express at Heaton Norris. Royal Scot 4–6–0 46106 'Gordon Highlander', with BR windshields in charge. 28/3/59. *Photo by Douglas Doherty.*

when it was necessary to remove a pair of wheels.

Just a little further up this shed road there was a 'wheel drop', also hydraulic, this being used for removing pairs of wheels from large engines, briefly, this was like a lift, the defective engine would be 'set' on the drop, side rods removed, and the faulty wheels unbolted, the lift would then be lowered, two lengths of rail would be pulled into position at rail level when the lift reached the bottom of the shaft, this shaft was about twenty feet deep, the engine would then be drawn clear and the lift brought back to rail level, the wheels would then be rolled along very carefully by hand to the fitters' square.

Passing from No. 1 Shed, the set would pass the Foreman Cleaner's office, a small brick building, gas tarred from ground level to about five feet up, when it was white-washed to the roof, outside this office were neatly stored bundles of cleaners' ladders, a few barrels of cleaning oil and three steel drums used by cleaners to put dirty cleaners patches in. The Foreman Cleaner ruled

his charges with a rod of iron, (sorry Sid). Immediately behind the foreman cleaner's office, is No. 2 Shed, first impression upon entering is, how comparatively quiet after the mad house of No. 1 Shed. The quiet belies the concentration of tremendous power which one beholds, for here are to be seen examples of all the motive power on 'The West Coast Route', 'Duchess Pacifics', 'Fowler Scots', 'Stanier Rebuilt Scots,' 'Baby Scots,' both original and re-builds, one would see 'Princess Pacifics', 'Stanier 5XP's' and a few of those 'maids of all work', the celebrated 'Black Fives', indeed a pedigree stable, if one may use the expression.

The set of men would arrive at the engine they are to prepare, no. 6110, the driver remarks "I notice they haven't re-built her yet".

Climbing on to the footplate, the first job is to put the 'blower' on a little bit to clear the smoke off the footplate, next to check the boiler gauge glass for water and simultaneously look at the steam pressure gauge. All is well, so the driver gets the oil bottle and will go to the oil stores for some 'G' oil, a medium grade of oil suitable only for cool running bearings. The allocation of oil for a 'Scot' from Crewe to Glasgow would be about six pints.

The Oil Stores is a large two storey building where everything except engine tools are stored. Various oils are kept in very large square tanks, these tanks are painted L.M.S. red and are trimmed neatly with black and white beading. They have internal steam heating pipes and oil is drawn off as required through large highly polished brass taps, there are drip trays along the front of the tanks.

On arrival at the stores, the driver will place his metal oil bottle on the steel counter at the stores window and shout "6110, 12.1 Glasgow". He will receive his allocation of oil and will then say "give us a rag and a few corks please", these are there for the asking but the oil has to be booked out. By the stores window is a large ball of 'worsted', this is used for making oil trimmings and also as a wick in a 'flame torch', there is also a roll of asbestos string and a gallon can of paraffin for use of shed staff.

Before going for the tools, the fireman will spread the fire all over the firebox, to do this he will get the 'paddle' from the fire iron rack which is on the tender, a paddle is a clinker shovel with a metal handle about twelve feet in length, other fire irons are known as a 'dart' and a 'pricker', the dart is used for breaking up clinker and for letting air into a big fire, it is like an over-sized domestic poker with an arrow head. The pricker is used for pulling clinker from the front of the firebox, it would also be used 'on the road' for pulling the fire through when the engine was not steaming freely. The pricker is a straight iron rod with the bottom six inches at right angles to the main length, all the fire irons are the same length, there are shorter ones for shunting engines.

After spreading the fire, the fireman will go to the tool hut for the engine 'tools', this is a bucket containing four sizes of spanners, a boiler

London Road Station, Manchester, in the process of becoming Piccadilly Station. Awaiting departure for Crewe and Euston is 46156 'The South Wales Borderer'. *Photo by Douglas Doherty.*

gauge lamp, tin of fog signals, hand brush, a flame torch and a tallow pot. He will also get two head lamps, a fireman's shovel and a coal pick, before leaving he has to check the date on the 'fogs' and make sure that the seal is intact, with the bucket and shovel in one hand and the coal pick handle slid through the headlamp handles in the other hand, it is a simple matter to walk back to the engine where he will arrive about the same time as the driver with the oil.

The flame torch is then lit. A flame torch is a crude but none-the-less efficient hand light, it is something like a small Aladdin's lamp in appearance, it is superior to an electric torch for oiling engines as it gives a greater area of light and it can be held against the tallow pot in cold weather to make the oil run better. After first putting the engine in forward gear, the driver will proceed to oil the side rods and valve gear on the outside of the engine, he will make a start at the left intermediate buffer, he will go along the left side of the engine pulling every cork out as he goes pouring in about an egg cup full of oil and replace the cork by giving it a press and two turns, he will throw away any corks which are worn or gone soft and insert new ones in their

place, if corks are screwed too far into their housing, they will severely restrict the feed of oil to the bearing surface, they will also be much more difficult to remove next time the engine is oiled.

The driver will cross in front of the engine and work his way back down the right side doing exactly the same, as he is oiling he also makes a mental check that the engine is safe to travel, he will be looking for things like bent side rods and broken springs. He will go down the right side of the tender oiling the axle boxes, at the back of the tender he will put a drop of oil on the buffer plates and rub it over with a small plug of cotton waste. A small amount of oil is put on the coupling and vacuum hose and carriage heater pipe are checked that they are in good condition, the driver then goes forward along the left side of the tender oiling the water pick-up and axle boxes. It sometimes happens that an axle box is found to contain water, the drill then would be to get the 'big spanner' out of the tool bucket and take out the drain plug in the bottom of the axle box, run off the water and oil, replace the drain plug and put a quart of clean oil back in. There now only remains the worm drive of the water pick-up

*Top (opposite page):*
First Stanier 4–6–2 6200 'The Princess Royal' running into Crewe in 1933.
*Photo by W. Potter.*

Royal Scot 46149 'The Middlesex Regiment' accelerating the up 'The Emerald Isle Express' away from Rugby, 25/4/59.
*Photo by Douglas Doherty.*

to oil, this is situated behind the leading tender steps. It is of great importance that the water pick-up gear should be in good condition, as water tanks are rarely below half full when a train takes water on the troughs. It is only necessary to skim the top of the water, to do this the dip is lowered to its full extension and immediately and without any pause at all, it is wound up again until the water can just be 'felt', the 'dip' handle is kept on the move by half turns up and down and a watch is kept on the tank gauge situated immediately above the dip handle. As soon as the gauge shows within 250 gallons of full, the dip is pulled up altogether, the result is a completely full tank and no flooded footplate.

If one were to pause at all even for a second on the initial dipping, the dip would lock itself in and it would be impossible to pull it out until one got off the troughs, the result of this would be a footplate flooded with water and coal, also it would empty the troughs and on a main line with a heavy concentration of traffic, could cause a following train to stop 'out of course' for water, with the result that trains following are stopped, thus making for inconvenience all round.

While the driver has been doing his work, the fireman has been doing his jobs on the footplate, first job is to light the headlamps, check the lenses for cleanliness and put a red shade in the front of one of them, having done this, the right hand boiler gauge glass cock will be shut off, the glass protectors will be removed and cleaned along with the gauge glass, a 'keen type' of fireman would put some silver paper on the back of the protector before this was put back in position, this will cause the water to show up much better, the gauge glass drain cock will now be

opened and the stop cock opened half-way to blow the gauge glass through, the drain cock is closed and the stop cock fully opened, note being taken that the gauge glass gland nut is not blowing, as this is a warning that the gauge glass is probably about to burst, no need to worry, as it would be a simple matter to close the stop cock and get a new glass put in.

The gauge lamp will now be lit and fixed in the bracket at the side of the boiler gauge glass, the tool bucket is to be put on the front of the tender by the fire irons and the coal pick to be placed on the 'flat' over the tender doors, these are safe positions and the equipment is readily available on the road.

All the time this work was being done, the steam pressure has built up steadily and there will be enough steam to test both injectors, a small amount of coal is shovelled all over the firebox to make a good hot base for when the firebox is filled nearer to train time. Most of the top link firemen would prefer to put the main fire on for themselves.

By the time the work is done on the footplate, the driver will have done with the oil bottle, so the fireman will take the oil bottle, tallow pot, hand brush, big spanner, flame torch and with some corks in his overall pocket and some cotton waste, he will go to the front of the engine. Here, he will leave the hand brush and the big spanner on 'the foot framing' and get down into the pit. If the front shackle is hanging down he will screw it up and fold it back over the coupling hook, this looks much more tidy than a loose front shackle, which, swinging wildly on the road, looks what it is, a mess.

Oiling underneath is commenced by doing the

four bogie corks, these will take about half a pint of oil each. Proceeding in a crouched attitude further back under the engine, it will be necessary to wipe a way up into the inside motion, as surplus oil gets flung along the bottom of the boiler and then drops down all over the motion, brake bars and inside the main frame, however, it is worth a lot to know where to wipe, as one could spend time cleaning where there was no need.

Having refilled the tallow pot from the oil bottle, this is placed on the leading brake bar, the fireman now climbs up the left side of the 'middle parlour' with the flame torch, this is rested on the inside con-rod and he bends down to pick up the tallow pot. All the corks on inside motion can be oiled from the middle parlour if the engine has been 'set for oiling', the valve gear being the same as on the outside except for the cross head, which, on a 'Big Scot' is in two parts, each part in its own slide bars, the small end of the con-rod is between the two parts of the cross head.

The inside slide bars are lubricated through 'worsted' tail trimmings, these tail trimmings are in a large brass oil cup situated on the left foot frame immediately behind the smoke box. The inside big end revolves round a heavily cranked leading driving axle which is balanced with some really hefty crank webbing known to loco men as 'tumblers', these tumblers are painted bright red, the task of oiling underneath an engine would take about ten to fifteen minutes.

It has always been accepted practice on the former L.N.W., that the fireman oils the inside motion, and, as it is a driver's responsibility to oil an engine, a young fireman is shown how to do this by a driver, the safety factor could not be over-emphasised.

After the inside motion has been oiled, the 'top' now has to be attended to, 'top' being the oil cups and mechanical lubricators situated on the foot framing, footframe is the platform extending round the bottom of the boiler. There is not much to this point of the job, small brass oil cups which oil the axlebox slides through tail trimmings, a large oil cup which oils the inside slide bars, there is also a pair of mechanical lubricators, one which it is the engineman's job to fill, oils the driving wheel axles, this will take about a quart to 'top up'.

The other mechanical lubricator, which lubricates the piston valves and pistons, is a fitter's job

to fill, this one is filled with 'Black Oil', a heavy heat resisting oil, very messy stuff to deal with, the engineman has to check that this lubricator has been filled, if not, the hinged lid is left open to draw attention to this fact.

These mechanical lubricators are of cast steel construction, they are about two feet wide by one foot long and are situated on the right hand of the footframe, the important thing is not to overfill them, or they become air locked and will not work. While he is on the framing, the fireman will open the smoke box door and examine the inside, a quick survey will reveal anything amiss, such as leaking tubes and washing out plugs blowing, also that it has been cleared of all smoke box ashes. The smoke box door is closed and the lugs round the edge of the door are screwed up 'really tight' with the big spanner. This is most important, as a loose door could cause a 'blow back' from the firebox and it will definitely affect the steaming of the engine, one remedy on the road when an engine is not steaming freely, is to 'give her a good leathering', loco slang for working the engine heavily, however, if this is done when the smoke box door is drawing air, it will cause smoke box ashes to glow and these burn the lower half of the smokebox door, making it red hot. When it goes cold after the run it has a rusty appearance and the engine is viewed with suspicion as to her ability to steam, by the next set to take her off the shed, all this just because the smokebox door was not screwed up 'really tight'.

After doing this job correctly, there only remains a few smoke box ashes to brush off the front of the framing and the set of men will get back on the footplate.

The fireman will take the coal pick and climb up onto the tender to trim it and break up all the big lumps, the coal will be stacked well against the sides of the tender to allow for topping-up when the engine goes off the shed towards train time.

As the fireman is doing this work, the driver will be oiling the brake, to do this he will get the big spanner and screw in the steam supply stop valve, he will then get the 'brake spanner' and open the plug in the brake oil cup, this cup does not require much oil, the brake oil cup is a round brass oil cup situated on the front left side of the footplate, after oiling, the plug is screwed up and the stop valve is opened, spanners are put back into the bucket along with the tallow pot. To test the brake for leakage, the driver will create twenty-one inches on the vacuum gauge by opening an ejector and then closing it, a note being taken how long the vacuum gauge remains at twenty-one, it should take at least five seconds before it begins to fall back to zero, any variation from twenty-one inches on the vacuum gauge will be reported to the foreman fitter. After testing the brake, the sanders will be tried, this is a simple test of opening the sand valve on the footplate and observing that sand is being blown under the front of the driving wheels. Having done this, all that remains now is to put the engine in middle gear, close the dampers, close the blower valve, the hand brake would have been on all the time the engine was being prepared. When getting off the footplate, the headlamps would be placed on their respective brackets, one at the front and one at the back. The engine would be left then until the train men came to take it off the shed.

As the set of men walk away from the engine, the two 'sandmen' come trundling by with their large two-wheeled wooden truck, this truck is laden with spouted buckets of clean dry sand, one man in the shafts pulling and the other pushing from the back. Crewe is one of the few sheds where full-time sandmen are employed, one could hear the rattle of their truck and buckets at any time of the day or night as they went noisily about their seemingly endless task, one sometimes wondered whether engine sand boxes were bottomless.

Continuing through the shed towards the mess-room, the set of men meet a jovial and clean-looking fireman, he is carrying a 'double trip food basket', after greetings are exchanged, the jovial one enquires what engine the set have been getting ready, the driver replies 'down postal' and adds that there is only the foot plate to brush up, the jovial one thanks the preparers and goes on his way, the preparing set indulge in small talk and arrive back at the messroom, where they wash their hands. They find one of the other sets of men are already back in the messroom, these are the set who went out to get 5703 ready for 1.50 a.m. Barrow, the third set will not be in yet as more time is allowed to get a 'Pacific' ready, normal 'prep.' time is one hour, one and a half hours for a 'Lizzy'. All the engines working north on Anglo-Scottish express trains are prepared for trainmen.

After about ten minutes, the outside man puts in another appearance, he enquires of the two drivers if the two engines just prepared are alright and receives an assurance that this is so. He then gives the first set a short list of engines to prepare, 5512 'Bunsen' for 2.5 Carlisle, 5736 'Phoenix' for 4.0 a.m. Euston and 5282 for 4.10 newspapers to Stoke, the outside man then goes on to say that 5512 is 'wrong road about', the train men are Carlisle men, double trip, and they can turn before they go off the shed. He then says that when these engines are ready the set can get their food and after that, have a walk across to the station to relieve the 'first Perth' due in at 3.40 a.m. The other set of men will receive similar instructions.

Having first looked at 'the board' to see where the engines are 'stabled', the procedure will be the same as for the first engine prepared, except for the Class Five.

5512 is a re-built 'Baby Scot' which makes them very similar in appearance to a re-built 'Big Scot'. Structural differences are the cab which has sliding side windows and the tender, which is all welded, they also have rocking grates and modified valves and pistons, this last makes them much faster engines, and they are more comfortable to ride on than the Scots.

The other engine to prepare is also a re-build, this time a 5XP, there were only two of this class re-built, the other being 5735 'Comet', the chief difference between these and the originals being a larger boiler and a double chimney, original cabs and tenders being retained, these re-built 5XP's do not have rocking fire grates and they would, like the re-built 'Scots', leave the originals at the post.

There is now the Class 5 to oil before the set of men have their meal break, this class of engine is simplicity itself. They are known as 'Black-uns' to enginemen, an engine that the L.M.S. have and other Companies would like to have, suffice to say here that very little, if any work, is beyond their capabilities, rarely indeed are these engines guilty of capricious behaviour.

Meal time is news time in the shed messroom, a time for discussing wages, politics, births, marriages and deaths and, of course, any local scandal going about the town, those women in the fish queue having got nothing on the sheddies when it comes to gossiping.

Other loco men in the messroom are two sets of 'shop shunt' men, their job is to marshal train engines in the right order for going off the shed, they also 'set' engines for the fitters, 'shop' drivers are old hands who have given up their turn on the main line.

There are four 'steam raisers' in the mess-room, these worthies are responsible for lighting up engines which have been stopped, for boiler wash-out and repairs, industrial fire lighters are used for lighting-up and an engine would be allowed six hours to get 'in steam' from cold. If an engine is wanted earlier, a spare fireman is given the job to 'purge' them, when this happens, an engine will make more smoke than the 'Queen Mary'. Steam raisers also look after stabled engines.

Also in the messroom are the two sandmen, who were seen at work earlier in the night and the 'examining fitter', an old hand fitter, he spends much of his time stooping and going from front to back underneath engines, tapping with his long-handled hammer, eternally searching for cracks in frames and axles, another part of his equipment is a very powerful electric hand light,

he is to be heard sometimes whistling, sometimes cursing, always hawk-eyed, he misses nothing, his is a very responsible position and no engine will go off the shed until he signs his name in the engine book to confirm that it has received his attention.

There are in the messroom, a few engine cleaners, they are a boisterous lot until the fore-man cleaner opens the messroom door at the end of their hour, when they go out very quietly. The foreman cleaner does not speak, he just stands by the door with half a smile on his face and does a count of his charges as they file out, quiet they may be, but it is only like the calm before the storm, for, as soon as they get back to their respective engines, they are at it again, singing, passing uncomplimentary remarks about each others work. The cleaners work in gangs of six, a gang will clean one big engine and a smaller one during a shift. Cleaners are sometimes used for 'knocking up', and to look after 'fire devils' at water columns during severe weather.

It is whilst these youngsters are cleaning, that they will learn the correct way to hold a fireman's shovel and how to 'put a fire on' in the proper manner. If they are working in the vicinity of an engine preparing to go off the shed, it will not be many minutes before one or two of them will

46133 'The Green Howards' in the company of 46257 'City of Salford' entering Crewe North MPD after works overhaul. 16/3/59. *Photo by Douglas Doherty.*

be enquiring of the fireman if they can put the fire on for him, he most probably will tell them 'to fill her up under the door', they will almost certainly put more coal on the footplate than in the firebox, still, everyone has to learn and a bit of tuition helps to put matters right, this is inexpensive training for them as they will also learn how to operate the various types of injectors and how to 'black the front' and get a footplate shipshape quickly and efficiently.

Having had their meal and a smoke, the driver suggests that it is time to have a walk across to the station to 'see how he's doing', they will go across the long iron footbridge, which is a direct link from the North shed to any of the platforms. As they are walking over the bridge, they see 'The Irish Mail' coming into the station from the Chester Line, headed by Scot 6112 'Sherwood Forester', the glare from the firebox lighting up the dawn sky like a powerful searchlight. The driver on the footbridge remarks that 'The Mail' is late and wonders what's been stopping him as the weather is not too bad to affect the boats. The set of men then go down the steps and go to the telegraph office window on No. 4 platform, in this window is a train reporting board, on which are shown passing points and times of all passenger trains coming towards Crewe from the North, thus one can see the progress of any particular train. The set of men notice that the train they are interested in was '12 late Preston' but was only '5 late Warrington' and the driver remarks that he should be 'right time in'. As there are a few minutes to spare, the set make their way into the Traffic Inspector's Office, situated next to the Telegraph Office, a small office, there are pigeon-holes on the walls and books and a telephone on the well-worn desk. At this desk sits the traffic in-spector, who greets the set, the greeting is ac-knowledged, whereupon the 'traffic' man says "What you after, the first Perth?", the driver confirms this and the traffic remarks that 'he's getting close to', the conversation then turns to the night's work in general and the driver enquires "What has been up with the 'Irish'," the inspector replies, "Customs having a bit of a purge at Holyhead, I suppose in about three months I shall be getting skins (skins, report forms,) wanting to know about the delay when its nothing to do with me". As he finishes talking, the inspector's telephone rings and is at once picked up, the conversation on the 'phone goes:-

"it is, ah, yes, up four, right, thank you". He then replaces the 'phone and turns to the driver and says "That's North junction, yours is next up four". The set bid the inspector "Good Morning" and go out of the office towards the south end of the platform as the station amplifier announces the destination of the next train to arrive at No. 4 platform, at the end of the announcement, the set of men's attention is attracted by the sound of an engine 'blowing-off' in the 'bank engine sidings' at the end of the platform. This is engine 5736 'Phoenix' prepared by the set earlier in the night and now snorting and raring to go.

Looking back towards the north of the plat-form, the set of men see the train approaching them, there is a muffled roar and a flash of brilliant firelight against the brickwork of the public over-bridge and 6225 'Duchess of Gloucester' comes gracefully to rest, mild warmth radiating from the boiler, the engine stands like a huge athlete after a long hard run. Immediately, the fireman of the set will take one of the headlamps from its bracket and will put a red shade in the remaining one, he will then hurry to put the lamp on the tender bracket and get down to hook the engine off, there is not much in doing this, it can be done in about two minutes and the fireman gets on the footplate before the trainmen have got off. On reaching the footplate, the intense glare from the firebox is momentarily blinding, the driver who has worked the train in is saying to his relief "There's nothing up with her, she's a good 'un, I am going to see *him* to see if we can have her again tonight" ('him' being the foreman fitter.)

The train fireman asks the relief fireman if he will put his shovel in the stores, he says he has chalked his number on it. Top link firemen usually stick to the same shovel, one with a big blade and well balanced and with this last request, the train men get off the footplate, and, each carrying a 'double trip basket', walk across to the shed to book off.

The relief fireman takes note of how much coal has been used and then has a look into the huge square firebox, he sees that the 'brick arch' is literally white hot and the slight metal content from the coal is running from the arch and down the front of the firebox. There is not much depth of fire, as this would have been run down on the last few miles into Crewe. The signal at the end of the platform would now show a 'proceed' aspect and the engine would move gently forward, passing close by 5736 which is about to 'set back' onto the train in the platform, up to the South junction where it comes to a stand behind a shunt signal, whilst they are waiting for this signal to 'come off' a 'through train' comes up past them, just starting to 'pick em up' after coasting through the junctions and station, there is no mistaking the 'beat' of a Stanier Pacific. The fireman of the relief set sees the number of the engine is 6249, 'City of Sheffield', and the driver says that "they are Cockneys on the St. Enoch's Sleepers" and adds that "they are timed to pass the Perth here".

The shunt signal 'comes off' and 6225 sets back down a 'through road' on to the Chester line and arrives at 'The Shed Bank Cabin' at the North shed, the engine is booked on to the shed here and the driver is given a time and told which road of the 'coal hole' to put the engine. As the engine is going to work the 10.20 a.m. to Shrewsbury later on, she will be put on the 'back road', there is always a long line of engines on this road waiting for coal, water and to have the fire cleaned and smoke box emptied prior to being taken on to the shed roads for stabling.

An engine wanted for a job in a hurry would be left in the 'front road' of the huge corrugated iron clad coal chute. Engines that would want 'turning' would be left in the 'middle road'.

As engine fires are cleaned, the engine number is entered in a book and the firedropper signs his name to it, this is done so that if any time should be lost on the road and the cause is found to be a dirty fire, it can easily be traced back to the culprit (L.N.W.R. practice). After the fire has been cleaned and ash pans raked out, the smoke box is cleaned out, this is about the dirtiest job on the shed. The 'chimney ender' wears any old overalls he can get hold of, an old cloth cap pulled well down, a clean shed cloth pinned round his neck and a pair of clogs on his feet, he will tie string round his trouser bottoms and elastic bands over his cuffs. He uses a number ten pan shovel with a long wooden handle to do his work, as

might be imagined, this job is made much worse when there is a strong wind blowing, if ever a man earned his 'corn' that man is the 'chimney ender'.

Having left the engine they have just brought to the shed, with a full boiler, hand brake hard on, engine in middle gear, cylinder drain cocks open and blower off, both dampers closed, the tools and headlamps are taken to the tool hut for the tool man's attention, the shovel with the train fireman's number on the blade is put in a corner of the tool hut along with other marked shovels, no other fireman would touch it and it will be there next time the fireman goes off the shed.

On the way to the messroom from the tool hut, the fireman asks the driver if he had found what the delay had been north of Preston, the driver replies "Yes, they were right time till they got stopped at Kirkpatrick, a car had gone through the gates and stopped the job". While the driver goes up to the check office to book the engine on the shed again and put a 'no repair' card in, the fireman peruses 'the board'.

The driver is not away many minutes and when he returns he tells his mate "We have got to get 926 ready for 8.10 Derby and that will be us straight up". (Straight up i.e. finished). 926 is a Midland compound, there are only five of these at Crewe, they are used on local services like Crewe–Derby, Crewe–Llandudno and Crewe–Manchester. They are easy engines to prepare with the result that the set of men are soon back in the messroom.

Here, after yet another hand wash, they confer with the other sets of preparers and they find they have not had a bad night at all, five 'preps' and one relief, another night they might well get eight engines ready when sets of men are scarce and there are one or two failures amongst the engines. Still, that's the way it goes and has done for something approaching 100 years.

The set have now only to 'book-off', bid each other "Good morning" and go their separate ways.

# Remembering Tinplate

Showing signs of wear and tear! Early L.N.E.R. 4–4–0 tender locomotive

DO you remember Hornby Tinplate? You probably do, because if your childhood was spent in any decade between the 'twenties and the 'fifties, then Hornby 'O' gauge trains would have featured large in your life if you were at all railway minded. Especially at Christmas!

Do you remember those cardboard boxes, coloured curiously dull red, with black script lettering? Toyshop windows full of them! Those boxes felt excitingly heavy, especially if (could it really be?) there was a locomotive inside. None of your modern lightweight plastic, and no super detail, but those trains were the delight of many boyhoods, and started life-long infatuations with railways both real and model.

Do you remember the very realistic liveries and lettering which the Binns Road factory so successfully applied to the tinplate rolling stock? Even in the 1950's the colour schemes were pre-nationalisation—the famous 'Big Four' companies which had disappeared under the B.R. banner in 1948. Hornby were curiously slow to follow the modern prototype trends, and so our trains in the early 'fifties bore the familiar initials—L.M.S., G.W.R., L.N.E.R. and S.R. This did not worry us in the least, I seem to recollect. Life itself was slower and childhoods longer than they are today —there was little worry about up-to-dateness. Canberras and Comets could exist cosily in the same world as our strangely outdated Hornby coaches, and even the Festival 'Skylon' held more awe for us than Concorde ever will for the present young generation.

L.M.S. 4–4–4T. From 1920's era.

Do you remember how we defended our trains against all criticism? The revolting child next door had Dublo (a great status symbol in those days). The engines had the right number of wheels and propulsion was electric (mother thought this might be dangerous, and even we never dared to touch the centre rail!). No, we were not impressed. 'Scale' model railways passed us by, for there was an indefinable realism in the clattering of a tinplate train which is not present in our present-day 'OO' gauge. The heavy tinplate had *inertia*—it rolled right and, to our juvenile minds, looked at least acceptable.

Do you remember how it felt to wind up a Hornby engine? The key incorporated a track gauge in its handle, and one had to hold the locomotive firmly on the track while winding. The key turned with a smooth and strongly resisting action which was quite different to lesser contemporary clockwork toys. There was a 'quality' in this feel which did not go un-noticed. Winding was an action to be enjoyed and was replaced in later life by other sensations—the 'touch of a Broadwood keyboard or the subtle gearchange of a quality car.

Where has all this tinplate gone? Most has gone the way of all toys, but fortunately some survives. The last few years has seen Hornby and other tinplate being taken seriously by collectors, and a thriving Hornby Railways Collector's Association now exists. The photographs illustrating this article show just a few items from the collection of Peter Gomm, who has done much to foster interest in old tinplate Hornby through his series.

*Top:* Variations on the brake van.
*Centre:* Pullman Car "Iolanthe"
*Bottom:* L.M.S. Banana Vans.

Tinplate signal box.

A signal box "opened up" to allow a working lever Frame to be installed.

Great Western and L.N.E.R.

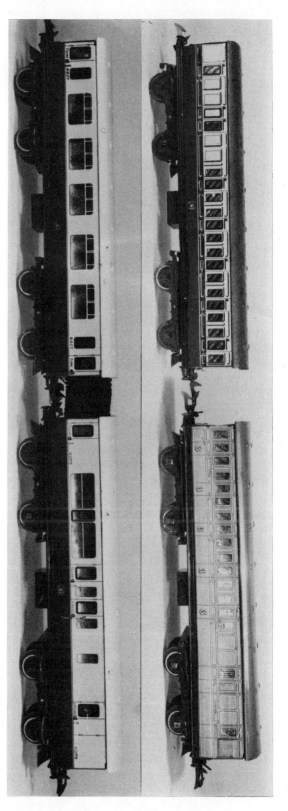

# "Footplate"

Driver H. Birkett coming off duty. He is leaving the footplate of an A4, after having handed over control to another driver, all at speed hauling the non-stop 'Elizabethan' from King's Cross to Edinburgh.
*Photo by British Railways, Eastern Region.*

Interior of cab 60022 'Mallard'
*Photo by British Railways, Eastern Region.*

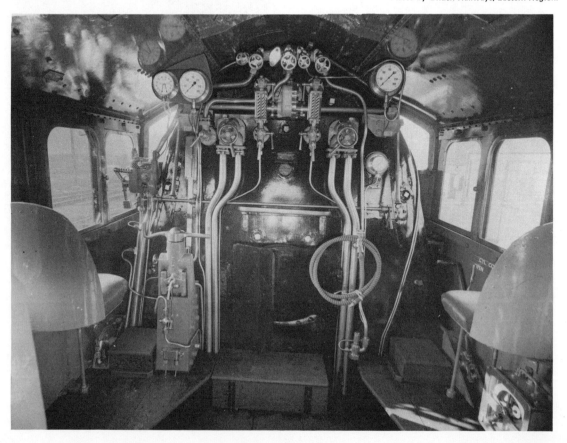

Cab of type AL.6 electric locomotive, built 1964/5.
*Photo by British Railways.*

"She's all yours", says Driver
H. Birkett on the left, handing
over the controls of the A4 to
Driver R. Currie. This changeover
takes place at speed on the
'Elizabethan' express non-stop
from King's Cross to Edinburgh.
*Photo by British Railways,
Eastern Region.*

# Gloucester, circa 1964

## by Norman E. Preedy

TO spend a day in and around Gloucester was always a rewarding experience for the railway enthusiast, even as late as 1964 when the writing was clearly on the wall, for the steam locomotive; Castles, Jubilees and even Royal Scots which had been displaced from other parts of the L.M.R. were able to 'rub shoulders' here.

Gloucester boasted two stations and two locomotive depots or, in enthusiast terms 'Sheds', one station was the Central which dealt with the Western side such as the Paddington services, also Cardiff and South Wales and Birmingham and Hereford. A vast amount of freight used this station and many trundled their way through to Wales during the course of a day, hauled in the main by a stream of grimy 2-8-0s and the larger tank locomotives of the 72XX, 42XX and 66XX classes to mention a few. Towards the end of steam, at the end of 1965 and early 1966, this traffic was largely placed in the hands of the very capable Midland Region Class 5 4-6-0s and Class 8F 2-8-0s. The Standard Class 9F 2-10-0s were also to be seen, because of the massive inroads made into the remaining stock of Western Region locomotives when during the end of 1965 an attempt was made to clear the region of steam haulage once and for all.

Possibly at the time of the early 1960s the main event at Central Station was the departure of the 8.18 'Cheltenham Spa Express' to Paddington which was the latter-day version of the world famous 'Cheltenham Flyer'. The train was brought into Gloucester from Cheltenham by a 2-6-2T and then handed over to a gleaming 85B (Horton Road) Castle Class locomotive more than likely 4085 Berkeley Castle, 5017 The Gloucestershire Regiment, 28th 61st, 5042 Winchester Castle, 5094 Tretower Castle, 7000 Viscount Portal, 7003 Elmley Castle or 7035 Ogmore Castle, all of which were then allocated to Horton Road Depot. Next, at approx 9. 30 a.m. came the through service from Cardiff to Newcastle which changed engines at Gloucester Central from a Cardiff (Canton) Hall or Castle to a Midland loco, usually a Jubilee or Royal Scot from Millhouses Depot (Sheffield), or even

a pair of Class 5 4-6-0s. Then of course came the minor services branch line to Hereford and auto trains to Chalford, both of which have long since been discontinued. There were trains to Leamington and Stratford and local services to both Cheltenham and Swindon. The Stroud Valley service to Chalford was usually powered by a Collett 14XX 0-4-2T and Horton Road Depot was allocated a supply of these locomotives; when a 14XX was not available an 84XX P.T. would be used.

Other incidents which aroused much interest at the Central Station during Sundays between October and March was the re-routing of South Wales trains through the station and also some of the through North/West services because of maintenance work in the Severn Tunnel. The Welsh trains were in the main powered by Castles and Halls from Old Oak Common Depot (London), Canton Depot (Cardiff) and Llandore Depot (Swansea) the latter being easily distinguishable because of their highly polished appearance and the Llandore 'trade mark' of painting buffer heads and smoke box hinges white.

North/west services were in the main hauled by a brace of Moguls, 63XX or 73XX and these came by way of the Hereford branch to Gloucester and thence to Bristol to continue their normal way West.

At various times throughout the year during the racing season Gloucester enthusiasts enjoyed the sight of special through excursions to Cheltenham Race Course Station for meetings. These came from all over the Region, again in the main powered by Castles and Halls. The big event in the racing calendar at Cheltenham was and still is the Gold Cup meeting held in March or April, Royalty attended this meeting which in its turn brought part of the Royal Train to Gloucester together with a brace of 'mint' Old Oak Common Castles.

At the second station (Gloucester Eastgate) passenger traffic was much in evidence and there was a regular service to Bristol and the North— Leeds, Bradford, Sheffield, York and Newcastle with local stopping services to Worcester and

Birmingham. The main services were the preserve of Bristol (Barrow Road's) allocation of Jubilees of which 45572 Eire, 45651 Shovell, 45662 Jervis, 45663 Kempenfelt, 45685 Barfleur, 45660 Rooke and 45690 Leander, were all common performers. Locomotives of the same class from Leeds (Holbeck) and Sheffield (Millhouses) were also to be seen.

In summer the Midland Station was of far more interest as there was a continual stream of trains from the North to the West Country seaside resorts. This special seasonal traffic brought uncommon locomotives to Gloucester which were not normally seen on passenger trains or in fact seen at all during the year. When the supply of Jubilees, Staniers and Standard class 4–6–0s ran out these extra trains would be powered by B1 4–6–0s from the Eastern Region, also Hughes Fowler 2–6–0s, Standard Class 9F 2–10–0s and on rare occasions Stanier 5 2–6–0s.

Other uncommon locomotives arrived in the Gloucester area on pigeon specials which came from places such as Manchester, Blackpool and Crewe, these trains brought Royal Scots to Gloucester and also Patriot Class 4–6–0s of both Unrebuilt and Rebuilt examples.

Gloucester is also supplied with a loop or avoiding line which cuts out the busy level crossings at either side of Eastgate Station, and allows a swift passage through for trains not requiring a stop in the City.

At the present time during the winter season the only regular passenger train to use the loop line is the Devonian which does not call at Gloucester. During the time under discussion the loop line was used almost continually during the summer Saturdays by passenger trains from North to South and vice-versa. Such trains would be Wolverhampton to Minehead or Paignton (which would be hauled by Castles or Halls from Stafford Road or Oxley Depots) and other through trains from North to South. During the night and on weekdays the majority of freight trains use the loop line. Even after steam had ceased on British Railways, Gloucester still saw steam in the form of Southern Pacifics and other Southern Railway locomotives en route from Salisbury to Newport for cutting up at Cashmores or storage at Woodhams of Barry. These locomotives would sometimes be stabled at Horton Road Depot awaiting entrance to the scrapyards and many would be the comings and goings of enthusiasts to record on film the passing of these great locomotives. Now the year is 1970 and Gloucester as a place of interest to the railway-minded is over. Once busy yards now lie derelict with weeds and grass growing up through the rusty rails, others have been ripped up and the sites levelled in preparation for new development not connected with the Railway. The Midland Depot has been demolished and the former Great Western Depot reduced to no more than a 'signing on point' whose only regular allocation is a handful of 350 h.p. shunters and a few North British D63XX locomotives outstationed from Bristol. The Central Station has been reduced to one through platform and the Eastgate Station to an island platform. The once proud signal gantrys have been taken down and in their place stand the robot type M.A.S. colour light signals. Such is Progress.

Avonside Engine Co. 0–4–0T 1104, introduced 1926 for dockside shunting. Danygraig MPD, Swansea 1958.
*Photo by N. E. Preedy.*

Powesland and Mason 0–4–0ST 1152 of Peckett design at Danygraig MPD, Swansea, 1958.
*Photo by N. E. Preedy.*

Peckett design for the Swansea Harbour Trust 0–4–0ST 1144. Danygraig MPD Swansea 1959.
*Photo by N. E. Preedy.*

Deeley 0–4–0T 41535 at Sudbrook Yard, Gloucester, for use in the docks. 2/6/62.
*Photo by N. E. Preedy.*

# The Railways of South Eastern England

## by Norman Harvey

TO deal adequately with the railways of South Eastern England in the compass of a single article is probably impossible; but nevertheless I shall try to show something of their difficulties, variety, and the challenge they set their Motive Power Departments. For my purposes, the lines under discussion may be taken as all those east of the LSWR's Portsmouth Direct route—that is to say, all lines owned by the South Eastern and Chatham and London, Brighton and South Coast Railways, together with the LSWR's route through Guildford, Haslemere and Havant. One or two smaller lines will be briefly touched upon—the West Sussex, Kent and East Sussex and East Kent Railways forming part of the Col. Stephens group, and the Southern's own working museum in the Isle of Wight. Now, alas, all these lines are electrified with the exception of the Hastings Direct line, and certain other branches which are operated by Diesel Multiple Units. Indeed, for steam passenger-carrying trains, one has to visit the Romney, Hythe and Dymchurch Railway in Kent. The Kent and East Sussex line has been the subject of a preservation attempt, but up to the time of writing (winter 1970/1) anyone wishing to see standard-gauge steam trains in operation must visit the Bluebell Railway in Sussex.

The lines under review, although diverse, faced common problems. The routes are nearly all short—under 100 miles and abounding in short start to stop runs and sharp gradients. Geographically, this is due to the need to cross the North and South Downs en route from London to the Channel ports. Although the first railway in the area was the local Canterbury and Whitstable of 1830,

'700' class 0–6–0 no. 308 on Bournemouth–Eastleigh stopping train approaching Totton. August 1937.
*Photo by R. F. Roberts.*

closely followed by the equally local London and Greenwich, the need for rapid communication between London and the South Coast, as well as underestimation by Parliament of the volume of traffic that would develop, led to both the London and Brighton and South Eastern Railways using the same tracks as the London and Croydon out of London. Here the track of the Croydon Canal was utilised as far as Norwood Junction, but it was impossible to avoid a two and a half mile climb from New Cross to Forest Hill at 1/100. It might be mentioned that this was the scene of a near successful experiment in atmospheric traction, which, had the method of propulsion not been ahead of its time would have easily eradicated the need for large scale electrification, the virus from which South Eastern England suffers today.

Although the remainder of the route to Brighton avoided any gradients more severe than 1/264, and the whole length of the South Eastern line from Redhill to Ashford was as nearly straight and level as possible, such neighbouring lines as that through Oxted were graded more severely, with an unavoidable stretch of 1/70 from Lingfield to Dormans, and the cross-country line from Eastbourne to Brighton faced the ascent of Falmer Bank, three unbroken miles of 1/88 through the South Downs immediately after leaving Lewes station. The London, Chatham and Dover Railway, built 'on the cheap' as a series of end-on local lines, likewise faced the five miles virtually unbroken ascent at 1/100 from Cuxton Road signal cabin up to the summit at Sole Street. The Brighton's own route to Portsmouth included about a mile at 1/90 between Warnham and Ockley, and the Portsmouth Direct, a contractor's line which the South Eastern very nearly took over, included ascents as steep as 1/80 near Haslemere and Liss. By complete contrast, the early and superbly graded London and Southampton Railway escaped without anything more severe than long sweeping lengths of 1/252.

But the challenge of the Southern lines produced a breed of hard-running enginemen, who would triumphantly storm the toughest bank and race away to break the sound barrier down the resulting hills. I shall be considering the work of Sam Gingell when I come to the section on locomotive performance, but Southern enginemanship was second to none. This should have been made plain to all comers in the last weeks of steam traction on the Bournemouth line, although outside my scope here. It is well known that drivers descended the gentle rise from Fleet as if they were making up time down from Stoke—these last steam runs from Bournemouth and Salisbury night after night, sometimes in appalling weather, set up as many reliably attested 100 m.p.h. maxima as may be found on any other railway in the country.

Perhaps the Southern's tragedy was that its designers produced the steam locomotive that could solve all its problems too late in the day. This happened twice. In 1930, Mr. Maunsell and his staff produced the magnificent 'Schools' class 4-4-0s when main line electrification was already being considered; and again, right at the end, the Bulleid Pacifics, some of them brilliantly modified to the designs of Mr. Jarvis, proved that a resolutely handled steam locomotive will equal most of the feats of its electric rivals. With net times of 56 minutes down to Winchester, the non-stop schedule to Southampton could have been cut considerably. I shall show how Sam Gingell made the time-honoured South Eastern sectional times look foolish. Of course the authorities refused to believe that it could be done regularly and by anybody. Of course it was, provided locomotives were well maintained and supplied with reasonable fuel. Bricklayers Arms burned Grade Two Welsh, Ramsgate their native Kent, but if quality fell, so did performance. This was nothing new. If Camden blundered and loaded the coal hopper with drums of oil, or occasionally firebricks, no trains ran until the matter was rectified. Electrification imposed uniformity; it also invited icing hazards over exposed portions of the line, and it cannot be said, by one who has made extensive use of them, that the present answer of third rail multiple unit traction is necessarily the right one. If you use multiple units, you lose flexibility; if your motive power unit fails, your train, or part of it, fails too. One imagines all this has been set against reduced turn-round time at termini, ease of maintenance and less complicated installations. One problem the Southern Electric did not adequately solve was supervision of staff, with a multiplicity of small depots from which early start-ups were often difficult. Perhaps there is no final answer to the problem of railway operation in the South East. The heavy suburban traffic, the Continental Boat Trains, the Airways Specials are all vital and useful, but they fluctuate, and the difficulty of surplus stock for which there is no adequate use through the greater part of the day is always with us.

At one time and another, I have spent many hours watching trains coming and going from the stations of South East England. They were a variegated lot, from East Grinstead built on two levels, littered with refreshment rooms and with flights of steps that of course lead you to the wrong train, to Lewes, grand junction for East Sussex, on an evening in high summer, waiting for the 9.2 p.m. slow to leave for Uckfield, the Newhaven C.2 throwing sparks in profusion when it mounted the embankment past the old station heading for the quiet of the Ouse Valley, and shortly afterwards the down Newhaven Boat Express would glide through, 'Atlantic' hauled and loaded sometimes at this season in excess of 500 tons; or again, on Friday mornings at Chatham, smoky and dismal, where in the halcyon 1930s one could book a first class single to Strood for three pence, and traverse the Toomer Loop in one of those distinctive South Eastern Saloons with individual arm-chairs. At Rochester, the 'jumper' would look in. "Can I see your ticket, young man?", he would say severely. When I proudly produced my First Class ticket, the first I had ever purchased, he would touch his hat, and say "Thank you Sir", a courtesy which I used to feel was well worth the extra penny it entailed. At Strood, too, was a refreshment room piled high with bottles where I used to ask for a cup of tea, to the disgust of the barmaid.

Alas, refreshment rooms in the South East are gradually being closed. East Croydon, remarkably, still has three, and Haywards Heath two, but the Brighton was always more lavish, or more civilised, than its neighbours. Waiting rooms are also suspect in modern eyes, and that, normally warm and comfortable, at my local station of Hayes, is up to let. Conveniences, too, are anathema; Pullman Cars are dying; and refreshment cars when they run are often unstaffed. Is there anything more sad than an unstaffed car? We are left with long barren platforms and trains that are lifeless and automatic. It was not always so. You could alight from your Hastings Express at Robertsbridge in Sussex and find in a nearby bay an ancient 'Terrier' waiting to take you to Headcorn, or High Halden Road; although it was left to the East Kent Railway to ply to and from Poison Cross. The West Sussex Railway from Chichester to Selsey closed in the 'thirties, but the Kent and East Sussex (which was an agricultural line) and the East Kent (which was built to serve the the coalfield) lasted into the days of Nationalisation. I knew the Kent and East Sussex best. It was said that if you were dismissed from the South Eastern, Colonel Stephens would give you a job, but the hours were long and the pay small. You did your own lighting up, and early rising was essential. But during the hopping season, the line was positively busy; and during the Second World War, when the Hastings Branch was blocked by enemy action, the important gypsum traffic from Battle was routed via Tenterden, and enough money was made for certain stations to be fitted with electric lighting, and for a 'Terrier' to be done up at Brighton works.

The Southern lines in the Isle of Wight were a working museum. As all the rolling stock had to come from the mainland, naturally it was transhipped only when needed. So the locomotives and coaches tended to become elderly; and the final stud of LSWR 0.2 class 0-4-4 tank engines became deservedly famous. I travelled over all the lines, noted all the locomotives in 1929, and as a result never felt the need to return until the last months of steam, when it was almost too late. The branch from Havant to Hayling Island was a 'Terrier' stronghold until the last, because restrictions over Langstone Bridge precluded the use of anything larger. They also became an institution, with a public house on the island named the 'Hayling Billy' and an engine kept as inn sign. They seem destined for virtual immortality. No. 72 'Fenchurch', built in 1872, is still working on the Bluebell Railway, as is her slightly younger sister No. 55 'Stepney' built in 1875 and there seems no reason why each engine should not reach her centenary. At one time 'Fenchurch' was owned by the Newhaven Harbour Company, and when the Southern took over that concern, reverted to the parent company. Thus, in preservation, she is lettered LBSCR on one side and Newhaven Harbour Co. on the other, which is confusing to say the least.

The traditional design of locomotive throughout the South East was the inside cylindered 4-4-0. The old South Eastern and Chatham owned nothing else, and some were of high efficiency. The Brighton owned only nine six coupled express engines—seven 'Baltic' tanks and two

H2 4–4–2 no. 32424 'Beachy Head' on 12.35 p.m. Leicester (London Road) Hastings train passing South Croydon. Sat. August 31st. 1957. *Photo by R. F. Roberts.*

G.W. 2–6–0 no. 6312 on 12.18 p.m. Hastings–Birmingham train passing Reigate. July 11th 1953. *Photo by R. F. Roberts.*

stately 'Pacifics'. Only the eleven Marsh 'Atlantics' that I used to think were some of the finest engines ever to run in the South stood apart from the general run of design, and Mr. Marsh came from Doncaster, as did Mr. Bulleid after him. For the rest, the Brighton had 4-4-0s or their tank engine equivalents, with the ageing 'Gladstones' which were a remarkably steady 0-4-2 design for certain secondary services. The South Western had some 4-6-0s, but in pre-grouping days mainly relied on the lively and handsome 4-4-0s designed by Adams, Drummond and Urie. It was left to Mr. Maunsell after the grouping to bring to perfection a 4-6-0 design for general service over the system—the well-known 'King Arthur' class could be seen anywhere from Ramsgate to Exeter. Carrying names associated so closely with the West Country, they were part and parcel of the Southern scene, but it is worth remembering that their designer was of opinion that they would not run any better for naming. Be that as it may, No. 777 'Sir Lamiel' held the Southern speed record of 90 m.p.h. at Byfleet until it was surpassed by 95 recorded behind a 'Schools' down Wool Bank. Although No. 850 herself is credited with 100 m.p.h. on test when new, the old Southern as such was not a fast line. No train was timed at an average of 60 m.p.h. The aim was to shift as large a load as possible at an average speed of 55 m.p.h. Steep banks and a congested suburban area precluded anything higher. The aim was timekeeping and reliability; and some sheds showed remarkable keenness in minimising delay. St. Leonards was a case in point, where lost time was almost unheard of.

One feature of the Southern scene that always attracted was the through trains from the Midlands, the North and South Wales carrying holidaymakers to their destinations on the South Coast. There was a Deal-Bournemouth through train, another from Plymouth to Brighton. Often unusual routes were taken—in Southern days the West London Railway was used for through trains from Manchester to Hastings and Margate, the steeply graded line from Redhill to Reading used for the Birkenhead to Dover service. The 'Sunny South Express' changed engines at Willesden (LMS to Southern), destination Brighton and Eastbourne; the Birkenhead at Oxford or Reading, and then on to Redhill, Brighton and Eastbourne. Reversals were common, and those pas-

sengers who liked a seat 'back to the engine' were understandably confused. So were those who studied the tastefully framed photographs of 'Scenes on this Railway' which adorned compartments, and might be surprised to note Windsor or Torbay whilst travelling between Eastbourne and Brighton. There was a twelve wheeled London and North Western Diner on the 'Sunny South', a refreshment car on the Birkenhead—the only such working over the Eastern Section, which was a Pullman Car line. All Pullman trains were a handsome feature. The 'Brighton Belle' (which still runs, although rougher now than of yore), the 'Bournemouth Belle', the short lived 'Thanet Belle', descendant of the famous 'Thanet Pullman', the leisurely 'Eastbourne Sunday Pullman', in steam days hauled by an L. 12 4-4-0, latterly composed of the spare 5-car unit from the 'Brighton Belle'.

Pullman Cars I think I miss most of all. It was pleasant to have a drink between East Croydon and Haywards Heath and argue with the conductor about the supplement; more pleasant, one Friday evening shortly after the last war had ended, to catch the 5.45 p.m. non-stop Lewes from Victoria, settle myself into the car, find I had unknowingly trespassed a regular passenger's seat, and to listen all the way down to bitter complaints: "He knew Sir Eustace Missenden", "Someone ought to write to the *Times* about it". People did write to the *Times* about an incident at Tunbridge Wells Central one Monday morning, when the leading enginemen on a double-headed up Hastings, objected to standing in the smoky tunnel. So they pulled up outside. The last coach of the train perforce stopped in the rear tunnel and being non-corridor went up empty. People were standing in the remainder! If sometimes, on looking back over many years of travel in the South East, one realises the passengers sometimes had a raw deal, for the enthusiast it was paradise indeed!

The South East was an enthusiast's paradise very largely because of the engines. Passenger rolling stock was variegated. I liked the new Electric main line stock for the Central Section, but it was sometimes unsteady at speed. The side corridor vehicles used on principal steam expresses was adequate, but when one ventured off the main line, and wandered down some branch in a SECR bird-cage set things were vastly different. The coaches were stiff on their axles, rode heavily

D Class 4–4–0 no. 31728 on 11.19 a.m. Brighton–Tonbridge train leaving Eridge. Fri. June 22nd. 1951.
*Photo by R. F. Roberts.*

D3 0–4–4T no. 2386 on Hythe branch train at Sandling Junction. June 1939.
*Photo by R. F. Roberts.*

T9 4–4–0 no. 287 on train from Salisbury at Southampton Central. May 1939.
*Photo by R. F. Roberts.*

'Schools' class 4–4–0 no. 933, 'King's Canterbury', on 11.23 a.m. Waterloo–Portsmouth and Southsea stopping train at Guildford.
April 1937. *Photo by R. F. Roberts.*

and were noisy; perhaps one's attention was directed more sharply towards the scenery, always delightful, or more often, was there enough standing at the next station for one to use the loo, as there wasn't one on the train!

The 3.55 p.m. from Victoria was a different proposition. From as long as I could recall, there had always been one corridor coach fitted with all amenities, and it divided at Eridge, where there was always an interesting afternoon period of intense activity in which four trains came and went in about ten minutes, and then quiet descended for the remainder of the day! The 3.55 p.m. was a long standing train bound for Brighton via Uckfield, and carrying a through portion for Eastbourne via Heathfield. For a time there was a van working on this train lettered 'Heathfield and District Poultry Association', which considerably dignified the ensemble. Many classes of locomotive were seen over the years, from Robert Billinton 4-4-0s and their rebuilt B.4X sisters, to the stately Marsh I-3 express tanks and his noble 'Atlantics'. My first footplate trip on this train was with Harry Thompson on 2423. I was hidden under the footbridge at Eridge until the coast was clear, and then invited hastily to step aboard. But the run of Harry's that I recall with most pleasure was behind a much-despised Maunsell U.I. "Why did Ashford want to give them three cylinders?" Harry used to ask. "Brighton did well enough on two".

Well, one war-time Saturday in March 1945 Harry Thompson booked on at Brighton to work the 12.18 p.m. stopping train up to Victoria via East Grinstead, and found the engine marked for the job was a Stewart's Lane U.I No. 1900. The foreman said she was too rough to take out; but Harry thought if he took her to London, something better might be offered in exchange. I don't know what he hoped for, perhaps a 'Schools' or 'King Arthur' fresh off works to shake them down in Sussex, but there was nothing and he had to do the best he could with No. 1900. She had a heavy train for this road of eight well-filled corridors. If he failed at East Croydon, all they had there was a coke-fired E.4 that would take at least an hour to reach Oxted; so he set sail and hoped for the best. If time was kept to Croydon, there was hope. As will be seen from the log, this was possible; but the engine was appallingly rough, run down and decrepit. But she would steam, the fireman was game and the coal (for

wartime) passable. So he set her to the climb through the North Downs like a mad thing. I can't imagine what cut-off he gave her, if the scale was capable of an accurate register. She was pushed to the limit, and coal was raining down on the carriage roofs and a great pall of smoke hung heavily behind us. We breasted the I/100 up to Woldingham at a minimum of 34 m.p.h. and raced away to 65 m.p.h. before applying brakes for the Oxted stop. 15 minutes 27 seconds—it wouldn't have disgraced an 'Atlantic', as my record was a minute faster with 2041 but hauling only five coaches.

Starting away, she sped down to Edenbridge in fine style, with an unexpected burst to 70 m.p.h. near Monks Lane, and time was actually being gained. But on to Eridge she was so rough that Harry had to restrain her. Passing over the Medway bridge at Ashurst she gave a sudden lurch; the fireman began to take a header into the river, but Harry grabbed hold of the seat of his dungarees and hauled him back. So we reached Eridge with all hands. Thence onwards, with a load reduced to only five coaches, things were easier. But time was gained throughout, and enough steam remained to attempt a superb climb up Falmer Bank, in which speed didn't fall below 30 m.p.h. on that long stretch of I/88. Brighton was reached five minutes early by the clock, and the despised Ashford product drew a word of commendation from her Brighton-reared driver. It was a great run.

I will close by recalling two runs between Chatham and Bromley South behind driver Sam Gingell, whose exploits have become a legend in his own lifetime. His friends sometimes feared that he would end in the river at Farningham Road; but beyond dislodging a few fragments of brick which were conscientiously gathered up by a Council road-mender in the valley below, all was well. The aim of course was the 'ton'. I never recorded it personally. Sam had it on his clock time and time again, when all I could record with a stop watch was about 95; but it was the spirit, the enthusiastic tackling of each run as it came that was the great thing.

When ten brand new Standard Class 5 4-6-0s came to Stewarts Lane, it was obvious that great things would be achieved, and my first run behind No. 73086 sets out the sort of experience that came my way on the Ramsgate Expresses night after night. With a heavy ten coach train, Sam

*Saturday 17th March 1945*                    3.55 *p.m.* VICTORIA–BRIGHTON

*3 cyl. 2-6-0 No. 1900: Load 8c: 270 tons full*
*Driver H. Thompson, Fireman Pearce (Brighton)*

| Miles | Point | | Schedule in mins | Actual time in mins secs | Speed in m.p.h. |
|---|---|---|---|---|---|
| | Victoria | Dep | | 0.00 | |
| 2.7 | Clapham Jc. | | | 5.55 | |
| 4.9 | Balham Jc. | | 9 | 8.47 | 34 |
| 6.7 | Streatham Common | | | 11.05 | 49 max. |
| 10.5 | East Croydon | Ar. | 16½ | 16.11 | |
| | | Dep | | 0.00 | |
| 0.9 | South Croydon | | 2 | 2.35 | |
| 1.9 | Sanderstead | | 4 | 4.16 | |
| 3.1 | Riddlesdown | | | 6.15 | |
| 5.0 | Upper Warlingham | | | 9.05 | 51 |
| 6.8 | Woldingham | | | 11.15 | 34/65 max. |
| 9.9 | Oxted | Ar. | 16 | 15.27 | |
| | | Dep. | | 0.00 | |
| 3.1 | Monks Lane Halt | | | 4.52 | 68/70 max. |
| 5.3 | Edenbridge Town | Ar. | 8 | 7.12 | |
| | | Dep. | | 0.00 | |
| 1.8 | Hever | | | 3.30 | |
| 3.7 | Cowden | | | 6.25 | 54/slack |
| 6.5 | Ashurst | | | 9.39 | |
| 10.1 | Eridge | Ar. | 14 | 14.11 | |
| | | Dep. | | 0.00 | Load 5c from Eridge |
| 3.5 | Crowborough | Ar. | 7 | 6.40 | |
| | | Dep. | | 0.00 | |
| 4.7 | Buxted | Ar. | 9 | 6.39 | 64 max |
| | | Dep. | | 0.00 | |
| 2.6 | Uckfield | Ar. | 4 | 4.15 | |
| | | Dep. | | 0.00 | |
| 2.9 | Isfield | Ar. | 5 | 4.34 | 62 max. |
| | | Dep. | | 0.00 | |
| 2.0 | Barcombe Mills | Ar. | 5 | 3.47 | |
| | | Dep | | 0.00 | |
| 3.8 | Lewes | Ar | 7 | 6.35 | 50 max Culver Jc. |

*Driver Sam Gingell, Firemen J. Williams (Stewarts Lane).*

CHATHAM–BROMLEY SOUTH

| Engine No. and Class | | 5MT 4-6-0 No. 73086 | | | D.1 4-4-0 No. 31145 | | |
|---|---|---|---|---|---|---|---|
| | Load | 10 cars : 345 tons full | | | 8 cars : 275 tons full | | |
| Miles | Point | Schedule in mins | Actual time in mins.secs | Speed in m.p.h. | Schedule in mins | Actual time in mins 'secs | Speed in m.p.h |
| | Chatham        Dep. | | 0.00 | | | 0.00 | |
| 1.4 | Rochester Bridge | 2½ | 2.55 | 30 | 2½ | 3.05 | 40/42 |
| 3.4 | Cuxton Road | | 5.49 | 44/48 | | 6.10 | 39/43 |
| 7.4 | Sole Street | 16 | 10.55 | 42 min 48 | 16 | 11 57 | 45 |
| 8.4 | Meopham | | 12.05 | 60 | | 13.05 | |
| 10.9 | Fawkham | | 14 17 | 80 | | 15.25 | |
| 13.8 | Farningham Road | | 16.13 | 94 slack | | 17 29 | 86/78 sigs stand |
| 16.9 | Swanley | 26 | 18.35 | 70 | 28 | 24.45 | |
| 19.5 | St. Mary Cray | | 20.47 | 70 | | 28.15 | 64/sigs |
| 21.2 | Bickley Jc. | 32 | 22.40 | sigs | 35 | 29.25 | |
| 23.4 | Bromley South    Ar. | 35 | 26.37 | | 38 | 33.56 | |
| | Net Time | | 26 mins | | | 30 mins | |

would set his engine at Sole Street bank, and on the run I tabulated it will be seen that he actually averaged about 47 m.p.h. over the 1/100 bank. On the occasion of my footplate trip on a similar train, he gave his Standard 40 per cent cut-off and pressure remained rock-steady during the climb. Then came the descent to Farningham Road, with speeds regularly above 90, and the current electric schedule would have been quite feasible had anyone thought fit to impose it.

The run behind No. 31145 is a Southern classic. These fine engines, the best of their size and power to run in Britain, used to work a Saturday afternoon train up from Dover that was popular with enthusiasts. Sam used to perform with his usual expertise, and the trip behind No. 31145 was an unofficial test run, to see how fast she could go. It was highly alarming for ordinary passengers, not interested in speed, as we tore away from Sole Street station with smoke drifting over the Downs and clinker falling around like hail. Although hauling two coaches less, there was only about 30

seconds difference in the climbing up to Sole Street, in itself a tribute to the wonderful D.1 front end. But down hill the cylinders would take steam faster than the boiler could generate it, and although over a short distance no adverse effects were noticed, in the long run performance would have tailed off. As things were a signal stand before Swanley, where we were well ahead of time, gave time for pressure to rally. So far as is known, this is the highest speed recorded behind a D.1 or sister E.1. It was a great tribute to a railway second to none in interest and fascination. Sam finished his career in a blaze of glory with the first rebuilt 'West Country' to come off shops, No. 34005. On his last run, he came down from Selling on a 'Boat' at 100 m.p.h. and the glasses on the counter of a lineside public house at Faversham bounced off on to the floor, so great was the vibration!

They were certainly the days, and I count myself fortunate in having seen so much of what went on.

C

# The X Section—a new slant on model railways from the U.S.A.
## by P. Mallery

IN the January 1969 issue of *Model Railway News*, L. E. Carroll described an excellent application of the principle of the automatic connection of power to a section of track. Proper application of this principle always simplifies the operation of a model railroad. On all but the smallest layouts, it is usually possible to install such automatically switched sections to advantage. Such opportunities are often missed because the possibilities are not recognised. This article takes a detailed look at the X (automatically switched) section, where it can be applied, and how it is connected.

Tracks candidate for an X section must meet two requirements. The tracks must be common to two or more routes, and they must be so located that it would never be desirable to leave locomotives standing on them for any length of time. The latter requirement means that X sections are short.

The first four examples illustrating applications of X sections are taken from trackage currently in service at the Summit-New Providence HO Railroad Club in New Jersey.

The most obvious use of an X section is a short track used to route trains between two parallel tracks, as shown in Fig. 1. There are nine possible routes through this X section, two of which are trivial. Since none of the routes can be used without one of the approach tracks, we can provide contacts which move with the points to provide power to the X section. In the case shown, power is obtained from the tracks on the left. It could just as well have been taken from the tracks on the right. To minimise the number of contacts, power is usually taken from the side with fewer alternative routes.

The contacts can be operated by the points, or by whatever drives the points, as indicated in Fig. 1. They may also be contacts on the panel switches used to control the points; electrically it makes no difference.

An X section with diverging routes at both ends is shown in Fig. 2. Except for connecting to tracks on the right, the wiring of this section is identical to that of Fig. 1. The contacts and their wiring in effect make the X section an extension of the track section to which the switches are set.

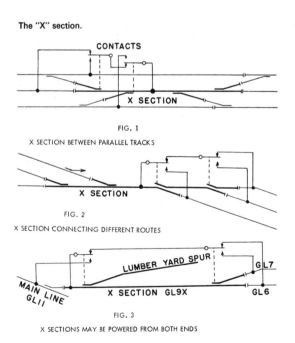

The "X" section.

CONTACTS

X SECTION

FIG. 1

X SECTION BETWEEN PARALLEL TRACKS

X SECTION

FIG. 2

X SECTION CONNECTING DIFFERENT ROUTES

LUMBER YARD SPUR

MAIN LINE GL11

X SECTION GL9X

GL7

GL6

FIG. 3

X SECTIONS MAY BE POWERED FROM BOTH ENDS

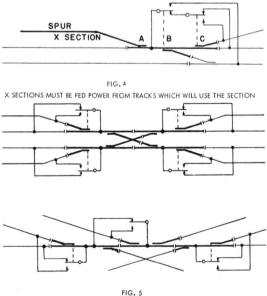

SPUR

X SECTION    A   B   C

FIG. 4

X SECTIONS MUST BE FED POWER FROM TRACKS WHICH WILL USE THE SECTION

FIG. 5

X SECTIONS MAY BE IN SERIES AND ONE X SECTION MAY DRAW ITS POWER FROM ANOTHER X SECTION

In most cases, X sections will obtain power from tracks approaching from one side.

Sometimes it is advantageous to connect to tracks at both ends of an X section, as shown in Fig. 3. In this case the wiring could have been simplified by making the spur part of the main-line section GL11. This, however, would have made the X section so short that it could not effectively be used for shunting moves between GL6 and GL7 without tying up the main line. Therefore, the spur and its switch were made part of GL9X, so all available track could be used for shunting with power being drawn from either GL6 or GL7 as appropriate.

In the cases shown so far, the X sections have had normal track on both ends, but this is not always so—X sections can be in series. To illustrate such applications, Fig. 5 shows two hypothetical cases. In the upper example each possible route (there are sixteen) uses two X sections, each of which is connected to one of the alternate tracks approaching it.

In the lower example, a route may use one, two or all three X sections. The two end X sections are like those shown before, and the centre one differs only in that when routed to the left X section it is *connected* to that section.

The examples shown all show the great advantage of the X section. In all cases they are tracks which may be used in rapid succession by a series of trains, each under a separate control. If they were powered as ordinary control sections, many operations of their electrical control switches would be required. But, as X sections, no electrical controls need be operated for them. This fact not only simplifies the task of the operator, but eliminates a fertile source of errors.

On an existing layout, there are two good guides to track which should be converted to the X section system. One is when the electrical controls are operated far more often than for the average section of the layout. The other is when a section often gets tied up for train movements which use only a small portion of the section.

Branch train at Killin Station. Killin was a branch off the Crianlarich lower–Stirling line, from Oban to Glasgow Buchanan Street Station. *Photo by Keith Pirt.*

Up express due to leave Bournemouth Central behind a pair of Electro-Diesel locomotives, nos. E6017 and E6022. 8/6/68.
*Photo by Alan Thorpe.*

'Merchant Navy' Pacific 35027 'Port Line' on a train at Victoria.
*Photo by K. Pirt.*

'King' class 6025 'King Henry III' on the down Sunday 'Cornish Riviera Express' approaching Cowley Bridge, Exeter. 14/6/59. *Photo by Michael Mensing.*

Down 'The Bournemouth Belle' leaving Bournemouth Central for West Station. In charge is re-built 'Merchant Navy' engine 35008 'Orient Line'. *Photo by Douglas Doherty.*

# Pressure on designers

## by W. A. Tuplin

Do we really need anything bigger than what we've got? Our biggest engines do our hardest jobs reasonably well. Now and again the heaviest express trains are overloaded so that we cannot be sure that they will keep time unless an extra engine is used. But isn't that more sensible than building a whole class of new engines big enough to take the peak load when it comes?

This was a recurrent question for locomotive engineers for over a century. A rational answer clearly demanded examination, not only of current requirements but also of probable future developments. Would the big trains continue to get bigger? Would there always be a need to make fast trains go faster? For a long time there were affirmative answers to these last two questions and they could help to justify a proposal that bigger engines of a new design be built for any railway. The Midland Railway was perhaps an exception as it held that increases in daily traffic between any two points should be countered by providing more trains rather than longer trains. For three ineffective years they even tried to run the LMS on this basis but it became clear that something different must be done.

The practice of providing more and more luxurious accommodation in long-distance trains ensured that weights would increase whether passengers became more numerous or not. On competitive routes, the booked times between the more important stations were always liable to reduction except where specific agreement between the competitors forbade it. So the power demanded of locomotives (at least of the locomotives that took the important passenger trains) was always increasing and so heads of locomotive departments had periodically to decide whether to accept regular double-heading for the hardest jobs or to build some bigger engines. Although the enthusiastic amateur admirer of locomotives was always pleasurably thrilled to examine details of any new design and although especially in later years, the appearance of a new design was regarded as a feather in the cap of the railway concerned, its development was not in every case a joyous task for the responsible engineer.

He had to decide what wheel-arrangement to use, how many cylinders to use, what size of boiler to build and so on. He had to estimate the weight of a locomotive of the new design and he had (on paper) to move the boiler backwards and forwards in order to find what position would enable the weight to be spread between the axles in a way that the civil engineer of the railway would accept. Relations between the locomotive engineer and the civil engineer were not always amiable and in bad cases, communication had to be made via the general manager. But even in the most favourable circumstances this part of the design procedure tended to be tedious. When at length a satisfactory design was achieved, the cost of building engines to it had to be estimated, and the advantage of the new design to the railway company had to be assessed. How much less expensively would it run trains in the current conditions? By how much would it permit this or that train to be accelerated? By how much could such acceleration be expected to increase the revenue of the company? This last question was not one for the locomotive engineer and indeed whoever answered it would have to rely a little

Inside cylinder crank and axle for Gresley Pacific engine.
*Photo by British Railways, Eastern Region.*

on guesswork which itself could be affected by emotion.

The classic example of technically unjustifiable development was Britain's first standard-gauge 'Pacific' the Great Western's *The Great Bear* of 1908. There was no operational need for such a large engine on the Great Western at that time or indeed for 25 years afterwards and no-one knows now why it was built. Among the more reasonable guesses is that someone persuaded the board of directors to believe that it would be a good thing for the Great Western to have the first British 'Pacific'. If the matter were handled rationally it would demand a proof on paper that the publicity value of *The Great Bear* was worth the difference between its cost and that of the Great Western's current standard four-cylinder 4-6-0 which was meeting all requirements with a good deal to spare. The circumstances surrounding the design of this first 'Pacific' made the job fairly easy for G. J. Churchward, the Chief Mechanical Engineer. The decision to build it probably emanated in the board of directors, and there was no operational need for it to be technically outstanding.

In general, however, the need for developing a new design was not accepted with pleasure by the locomotive engineer. He had usually enough to do in devising means for minimising the running costs of the existing locomotives doing their regular jobs. To have to start fiddling with something new to meet the demands or the forecasts of the traffic department within the restrictions of the civil engineering department was just another job that he could very well do without. When at length the first engine of a new design was to appear in public, he made sure that it was beautifully painted, with polished brass and gleaming mechanism, announcing to all the world proud triumph over the forces of Nature and of bureaucracy, while he himself was hoping against hope that the imperfections that he had been unable to avoid would not prevent the engine from being better than its predecessors. In some cases, of course, the difference in certain physical characteristics ensured that the new would be superior to the old in one or more respects and so would not entirely let its designer down. The Gresley 'Pacifics' on the Great Northern, for example, were bound to be better than the Ivatt 'Atlantics' in getting big trains on the move as they had some 50 per cent greater nominal ad-

Brand new off Doncaster Works. 60114 'W. P. Allen'. Peppercorn A1 class Pacific. *Photo by British Railways, Eastern Region.*

39

hesion weight. Even with allowance for the uncertain difference between nominal adhesion weight and actual adhesion weight, 50 per cent is a margin big enough to be pretty sure of showing itself. But whether the 'Pacifics' had such an advantage in running costs, or any advantage at all, over the 'Atlantics' in much of the work they did at first is doubtful and would have been difficult to demonstrate. What Gresley did demonstrate was that one of the 'Pacifics' could run a 600-ton train on one of the regular services where the normal load was about 450 tons. No attempt was made at that time to find out what an 'Atlantic' could do with 600 tons and subsequent events suggest that such an attempt might have lessened the lustre of the early 'Pacifics'. Only three years later, the Gresley Pacific design did in fact lose face in a contest that was (by the latest account) arranged behind Gresley's back. This emphasises that while locomotive design was something in which a Chief Mechanical Engineer might usefully take interest, his real job was to fight his enemies amongst the heads of other departments, and elsewhere.

How many engines of a new design should be built in the first place? With regard to the fact that every new feature is a potential source of

trouble, the obvious answer is 'One!'. This clearly minimises the waste of money on anything that has to be replaced because it is found to be unsatisfactory. On the other hand a batch of (say) six engines built at the same time will cost appreciably less per engine than does a single one. Moreover—and this is less obvious—it is possible for such minute care to be expended on all the details of manufacture of a single prototype as to conceal the fact that more realistic procedure may produce minute imperfections that can make all the difference between complete success and indifferent performance in service.

In this feature of locomotive development, perhaps the most dramatic incident was the order placed by the LMS late in 1926 with the North British Locomotive Company for fifty 3-cylinder 4-6-0s of a new and untried design subsequently called 'Royal Scots'. The circumstances were, however, unusual, as the operating department, acting behind the back of the Chief Mechanical Engineer, had told the management that it would not accept his ideas on main-line locomotives. As the management had set its heart on a big publicity 'splash' round a newly-styled 'Royal Scot' London–Glasgow train in the summer of 1927, it no doubt accepted the responsibility for placing such a large order for locomotives with certain antiquated features that ought never have been set on paper in 1927. Nevertheless the 'Royal

Re-build of L.M.S. 6399 'Fury', now 6170 'British Legion' at Edge Hill MPD.

*Photo by W. Potter.*

Photo of frames for Gresley Pacific. laid down in Doncaster works in G.N.R. days. *Photo by British Railways, Eastern Region.*

Scots' when new, were better than most other LMS locomotives of the time and so the management was satisfied until it brought in a later CME who was of course safe in condemning anything that originated before his arrival on the scene.

The years 1926–1927 found all four Chief Mechanical Engineers under non-technical pressure to do something technically doubtful. On the Southern they already had some good 2-cylinder 4-6-0s carrying, at the instance of the Publicity Department, striking names associated with the Knights of the Round Table, but something more notable was wanted for the heavier main line passenger trains. So the 'Lord Nelson' four-cylinder 4-6-0 with a 'gimmick' in the shape of four valve gears was built and was announced on the strength of its nominal tractive effort to be the most powerful passenger train engine in Great Britain. Swindon had clearly to reply quickly to this and therefore produced 'King George V' in a hurry. The need for speed forbade any design procedure other than enlargement of the proved 'Castle' four-cylinder 4-6-0 whereas some different thinking would probably have produced something better. The 'King' was too heavy to be accepted by the civil engineer in 1926 but under cross-examination by the General Manager who, impressed by the need for new publicity was personally interested in the matter, he admitted that in 450 miles of Great Western main lines only two bridges were so weak as to prevent the permissible limit of axle-load from being raised from 20 tons to 22½ tons. This was soon put

right, but no ordinary contact between the mechanical and civil engineers would have done it. Artificial conditions such as these were not conducive to rational design and Swindon's adoption, in emergency conditions, of the 'make everything a bit bigger' procedure in developing the 'King' led to a boiler pressure of 250 lb. per sq. in., also adopted for the 'Royal Scots'. Gresley followed the fashion thus instituted by producing 'Pacifics' with 220 lb. instead of his original 180 lb.

Many admiring students of locomotives and locomotive design are genuinely shocked at the suggestion that locomotive design was influenced by fashion, but examination of the history of the subject leaves no doubt on the matter. So long as new locomotives were used as items of publicity, every designer was likely to be affected in some degree by the normally accepted need to keep up with the Joneses. Because of the psychological impact of the phrase 'high-pressure' he tended to follow, regardless of technical considerations, any upward trend in boiler pressure. A regrettably large amount of money was wasted in building and running many British locomotives by the adoption of unjustifiably high boiler pressures.

A feature of steam locomotive development over a long period was the gradual introduction of 'refinements' so that design became complicated until someone realised this and stepped sharply back to simplicity as an ideal. Whale did this on the North Western in 1904, Urie on the South Western in 1913 and Riddles on British Railways in 1951.

# The Lincoln Branch of the Midland Railway

## —an outpost of Hudsonia

### by J. Cupit

THE Midland Railway, like many of the early companies, furnished itself with a heraldic device by using together the arms of the principal communities served. Of the half dozen cities thus honoured by the Midland, five were important railway centres on the Company's main lines; the sixth, Lincoln, was out at the end of a secondary branch. How, then, did the cross and fleur-de-lys of Lincoln find its way into the Midland crest?

In the summer of 1839 the Midland Counties Railway set up shop with the opening of a line from Derby to Nottingham. In the Midland Counties scheme of things—which took final shape a year later—Nottingham was served by a seven mile branch from their Derby–Rugby main line at Trent Junction. For several years the Nottingham station in the Meadows was destined to be a terminus; the Midland Counties and its disassociates, the North Midland and the Birmingham and Derby, were too busy slitting each other's financial throats in the traditional manner to undertake extensions.

But by 1844 necessity—and George Hudson— had caused these strange bed-fellows to sink their differences, and, 'with three cheers for railway amalgamation' to combine under the title of the Midland Railway.

The new company had little time to consolidate. Already to the west lay the nucleus of the unborn London and North Western; and even whilst the Midland shareholders were making the Derby welkin ring, schemes were brewing in other quarters for the building of a trunk line from London to York. This would not only be a powerful rival to the Midland's own round-about route to the North, but would form a barrier in the east which Derby would find it very difficult to break through

The Midland attack against this threat was three

fold. In 1845 they obtained powers to extend the Nottingham branch to Lincoln and also to build a line eastwards from Syston, on the old Midland Counties main line, to Peterborough. In the territory between these two was the independently-promoted, Midland-blessed Ambergate Company, planning to connect Nottingham and Grantham, a pawn in King Hudson's game, to be taken over at the Midland's convenience.

Hudson's moves met with mixed results. The Midland reached, but not, breached, the Great Northern at Peterborough; the Ambergate affair boomeranged disastrously, and brought the GNR not only to Nottingham but even to Derby itself! The Lincoln extension alone was successful, and to this day it is the only branch built and owned by the Midland Railway to seriously penetrate the iron curtain of the Great Northern main line. Small wonder then that the Derby Company included the Lincoln arms in its crest!

The branch was opened in the summer of 1846 and within six months had produced this vivid picture of rail travel in the early days.

"We were jolted just as if we were crossing broad and deep ruts, and at seven miles from Lincoln we came to a dead stop. The engine was so worn out and unfit for work that the fire in the furnace had actually burnt its way through the iron, and there were the hot cinders falling out as fast as they could, the water getting cold, and no longer any appearance of steam. Happily there was a drain near at hand, and pick-axe and shovel were speedily put into requisition, and a large tile extracted, which, broken in half, served to stop up the aperture. The posts and rails which fenced off the railroad were taken and broken up for fuel, and we at length crawled on to Lincoln......"

Thus from the pen of an Oxford man in 1847.

Sandringham class 61620 'Clumber' pulling into Lincoln Central with a train from the Eastern Counties to Liverpool.
*Photo by J. Cupit.*

* * *

The train indicator board directed us to Platform One, but the outer platform at Nottingham Midland Station was innocent of train on the dull January morning in 1957 I had chosen, with a fellow enthusiast, to make the acquaintance of the Lincoln branch.

"That's 'er—she'll be across in a few minutes," confided a friendly porter, nodding towards the centre road where a sombre-looking ex-Great Central Director No.62667 'Somme' simmered contentedly at the Lincoln end of a rake of five bogies. We sought the warmth of the Refreshment Room and recalled, over a cup of tea, the last time we had seen 'Somme,' lined out and immaculately groomed, rolling southwards with 14 bogies of the Farnborough Flyer one September morning in 1955.

Ten minutes before the advertised departure time, the D11 slowly set back its train into Platform One. In addition to the five coaches, the 11.23 a.m. all stations to Lincoln now consisted of a bogie luggage brake of incredible filthiness on the last stage of its journey from Colwyn to Lincoln, two vans of USAF mail destined for American airfields in Lincolnshire and two cattle trucks complete with bellowing bullocks bound for Boston. Our departure was delayed by the late arrival of the 9 a.m. Manchester (Central) to St. Pancras, with which we have an advertised connection. But the wait was not in vain; some thirty travellers from the north joined our already considerable passenger load and at 11.30 we set off on the 75 minute journey to Lincoln.

Our departure from Nottingham was nothing if not spectacular, for the Manchester train pulled out at the same time and for a quarter of a mile the Director and the Jubilee ran neck and neck until 'Raleigh' swung away to the south and St. Pancras. At first we picked our way through the yards and sidings of industrial Nottingham, passing to our left a J50 shunting sugar beet in the London Road Station of the former GNR, closed to passengers in 1944, now used as a goods depot. A mile out, the GN London Road–Grantham line crossed over us and kept company as we ran along at the foot of the tree-covered slopes of Colwick Woods, a local beauty spot being invaded by the builder.

At Colwick the two lines diverge; long ago there was a connection here, the Northern using Midland tracks to Nottingham, an arrangement which soon led to sparks and to the GN's independent entry into the city. Carlton and Netherfield (for Gedling and Colwick), 3½ miles from Nottingham, was our first stop and here we encountered the blue and white station signs of the Eastern Region, so it would seem that King's Cross has had the last word on the Lincoln branch after all these years! Beyond Carlton the Director hustled smartly along under the Great Northern's Colwick–Derby line; over us, in contrast, a W.D. 2–8–0 made a heavy going on a greasy rail moving a load of mineral empties out of Colwick Yard.

The delightfully named Burton Joyce (5¼)—the name is derived, not from some dainty damsel but from one Bertune Jortz, a 13th century knight—provided us with five passengers in exchange for three ladies, homebound from a Saturday morning shopping spree. We left the last traces of suburbia as 'Somme' moved us out

of Burton Joyce; ahead now lay the rich lands of the Vale of Trent, seen at its best in blossom-time.

The line follows the Trent closely, and except for two bridges across the river and a few small embankments near Newark, the surveyors were able to avoid construction work to such an extent that there was not a single road bridge—over or under—the 35 miles of railway between Nottingham and Lincoln! Today, on this line of level crossings, Lowdham (7½) is unique, for in recent years a modern fly-over bridge has replaced the old crossing.

We made halts at Thurgarton (9¾) and at Bleasby(11). At the latter a trio of schoolboys alighted, collected bicycles from the rather austere-looking shelter and had ridden off before we had resumed our journey—a fine example of road-rail co-ordination! Beyond Bleasby the branch from Southwell makes a triangular junction with the Lincoln line, and at Fiskerton Junction, where the west-to-north curve swings away, the crew of a light engine waiting to cross from the branch scowled at us as we passed—perhaps they had hopes of getting back to Nottingham in time for the F.A. Cup matches that afternoon.

On the base of the triangle is Fiskerton Station (12¾) and it is but a short ¾ mile run from here to Rolleston Junction where the eastern curve of the Southwell branch trails in. A crowd of workmen clattered down as our guard and the station

D11 62660 on Nottingham Midland–Lincoln train entering St. Marks Station. About to depart for Nottingham is 42161. 25/8/56 *Photo by J. Cupit.*

44

master exchanged gossip over the loading of straw-packed rose trees consigned from the nurseries of Southwell to a lucky gardener in Scunthorpe. The branch platform was deserted, for our train is one of the few with no convenient connection for Southwell.

A post-war power station on the banks of the Trent has brought an industrial flavour to the line between Rolleston and Newark; at Staythorpe Crossing box we passed an 8F 2–8–0. on the down road backing loaded hopper wagons into the new sidings. On the up side construction work for a further yard is in hand.

After bridging a turbulent Trent the Director was soon wheeling us over the Great North Road level crossing into Newark Castle Station; 'Castle' is a British Railways inspiration, though one hasn't far to look for the source, for across the river stands Newark Castle—now but a ruin—knocked about by the late Oliver Cromwell for its Royalist sins in the Civil War. The platforms of Newark Station are short and whilst we made our stop the mixed part of our train was out over the crossing, causing a fine hold-up on Britain's A1 road; but, despite a considerable exchange of passengers, the staff put in some smart work and within a couple of minutes the D.11 was slipping her way through Newark yards where a J39, in from Lincoln with the morning pick-up, waited to follow us out. Numerous maltings, engineering works and a sugar beet factory ensure a healthy goods traffic, and a $\frac{1}{2}$ mile, single line branch connecting with the Great Northern is used for freight transfers. A mile out of Newark the Midland crosses the GN main line on the level.

At Collingham ($22\frac{1}{2}$) we left the Vale of Trent— and a few local passengers from Newark—to head for the valley of Lincoln's river, the Witham. The watershed between Trent and Witham provided the planners with no problems for, after crossing the Nottinghamshire/Lincolnshire border, Swinderby, our next stop is the 'summit' of the Newark–Lincoln section—50 feet *above sea level*. In addition to the usual small yard at Swinderby, there are sidings into an R.A.F. Camp, providing extra traffic, both passenger and freight, for the branch.

Our last intermediate stop, at Hykeham, provided us with home-going workers employed in the nearby foundry. From here we ran through the new suburbs of ancient Lincoln; by works and factories, under the avoiding line of the Great Northern with a glimpse of a 9F 2–10–0 westbound from March on a mixed freight, curving round through the Midland West Yard to our journey's end at Lincoln St. Marks.

As we ran into the arrival side 2–6–4T No.42342 was ready to leave from Platform Two with a crowded 12.50 (SO) all stations to Nottingham; on shed slumbered the pilot, No.68602 of Class J69 in company with a filthy 'Zeebrugge', co-star with our own 'Somme' on the Farnborough Flyer adventure.

The Midland Station at Lincoln—St. Marks came with British Railways—is a two platformed affair with two centre carriage sidings, all under a single roof, and very reminiscent of those old engravings of the early railway stations. It was an impression heightened for us by the sight of a Royal Mail TPO van stabled on one of the centre roads. St. Marks was originally a terminus but within two years of opening the MS. and L. line from Grimsby made an end-on junction here, the Sheffield Company's trains using the Midland's station. The only regular passenger trains to run through St. Marks today are the up and down workings of the Cleethorpes–Birmingham service.

Most trains on the branch, some 12 trains each way daily, run between Nottingham and Lincoln of which several are through workings to or from Derby; in addition there are a few round trips between Nottingham and Newark only. The TPO leaves Lincoln at 8 p.m. on a through train to Tamworth where it connects with the West Coast Postals, arriving back in Lincoln at 4.45 a.m.

By 2.45 'Somme' had trundled the five vans across to Lincoln Central for forwarding, had turned, coaled and watered, and was coupled up to our train—now strengthened to nine bogies for the 3.5 p.m. to Derby. On the return trip it was all stations to Newark, a brief halt at Rolleston Junction, and then an exhilarating non-stop romp through driving rain and gathering dusk to a Nottingham Midland Station crowded with football fans.

Though no longer an outpost of Hudsonia, yet this line is an outpost still—against the bus. In these depressing days of branch-line closures it is heartening indeed to ride, as we had done, a byway of British Railways with as healthy a passenger traffic as that carried by the Lincoln branch of the Midland Railway.

# From Sheffield (Midland) in 1905

## by W. A. Tuplin

MOST boys have at one time wanted to be an engine-driver. They had seen steam locomotives moving passenger trains and goods trains fast and slow in all sorts of places. How nice it would be to control this quick and strong machine. How doubly nice it would be to get paid for doing it! Instead of going to school or struggling with hot heavy things in a steelworks or digging coal in the dust and dark of a coal mine, an engine-driver could be driving along in fresh air and going to London or Birmingham or York every day of his life.

Every young man who was resolved to realise that aim had first to become an engine-cleaner at a shed where locomotives rested between spells of train hauling. Other young men who may have lacked that sort of ambition but who knew that one worked or starved, and who didn't much mind the dirt, might also become engine-cleaners. So at any shed, the cleaners might be a very mixed bag but nevertheless, before World War I, they did very good work. Steam engines at work then were usually cleaner than those in exhibitions today.

A man might be cleaning for five years before he became a fireman on a shunting engine. He might serve for fifteen years as a fireman on a wide range of jobs before promotion to driver and he might be twenty years as a driver before he was allowed to take charge of long-distance passenger trains.

And the pay? Not very good, but the job was a regular one. If you did it reasonably well and behaved yourself the job, with its slow promotion, was there for life. Not every job in the early 1900s was safe, and if you lost yours there was no unemployment pay. You had to get along as best you could with the aid of friends or relatives who themselves were not well off, till you found something else.

An engineman's job was healthy at least to the extent that there was plenty of fresh air and exercise. When the engine was working hard over a long distance, the fireman had a great deal of exercise. If the driver thought that he could usefully have more exercise than his own job really provided, he could usually persuade the fireman to change jobs for occasional short periods.

What many people would dislike about an engineman's job was the wide variety of starting times and finishing times and (on goods trains) the large amount of night work and of lodging away from home on alternate nights. A man who had to leave home at 2 a.m. in snow and sleet in order to 'book on' at 2.50 a.m. might well be doubtful as to whether the job really was a healthy one.

Those men who had to leave bed at specially early times were 'knocked up' by a youth despatched from the shed on a round of such duties. The first care of an engineman on rising was to collect together his food for the day because none was provided at engine-sheds and indeed few enginemen had any chance to get to a shed except when 'booking on' or 'booking off'. Nevertheless enginemen were not absolutely restricted to 'cold lunch' as the fire and the shovel, during a waiting period, could cook quite well within their obvious limitations.

So with a basket of food and an enamelled can of tea an engineman on an early turn walked all the distance there was between his home and the shed in fair weather and foul. He booked on, read the notices about temporary modifications to the instructions for running trains over the route he was to travel, collected oil and perhaps a sponge-cloth from the stores and carried them to the engine. An hour was usually allowed for preparation of the engine, which included filling all oil-boxes, checking that worsted oil-trimmings were all right, checking the tightness of nuts in various places, and livening up the fire so that full boiler pressure would be reached by the time the engine reached its train. This work was shared by driver and fireman and if either of them was a 'strong character' he would no doubt contrive to do less than his fair share. If the engine were not under cover this work could be specially unpleasant in rain or snow, but even if carried out in the shed it was tedious and uncomfortable. Between sunset and sunrise the men carried 'duck lamps' of flaring oil to be able to see what they were doing.

What sort of engine might be used on the Midland in 1905 to take the first passenger train of the day from Sheffield to Manchester? Quite likely a Kirtley double-frame 2-4-0 (with some detail alterations or even rebuilding during its thirty or forty years' life) an engine that many enthusiastic amateurs admire. What sort of cab does it have to shelter its crew from the cold and wet of a winter's morning of falling snow and sleet? None at all! It has a weatherboard, a roof reaching back from it by about 15 inches, and side sheets that extend over the full length of the footplate at the bottom but are narrowed down to about 6 inches at a man's shoulder-height. On the North Eastern Railway each engine-cab was a little house that could be too warm in summer, but there was nothing like that on the Midland. On a bad day in winter you put all your clothes on and hoped for the best.

Many of the Sheffield-Manchester trains originated at Rotherham (Westgate) and the first regular one was due out of that station at 7.50 a.m. So the first 'leg' of the day's work was to run a few miles tender first perhaps into icy wind and snow and after that, running forward could feel quite warm. Indeed until the steam heaters got going in the coaches the passengers might be colder that the enginemen.

A steady plod up the 1 in 100 from Sheffield to the first stop at Dore warms things up for everybody and the engine's whistle on entering Totley tunnel sounds almost cheery.

On leaving Grindleford station at the west end of the tunnel, snow is no longer falling, and the daylight reveals a landscape of breath-catching black and white beauty that pervades most of the Hope Valley. As the engine does not need to be worked hard till after Edale station the enginemen could almost enjoy this if it were not so damned cold. But even apart from Cowburn Tunnel, little of the remainder of the journey to Manchester is scenically inspiring. The gradients make no demand on the engine, but the succession of starts and stops is monotonous and fatiguing and the men are glad to reach Manchester Central which at least has a roof.

Stanier 'Jubilee' 45668 'Madden' coasting to its Chesterfield stop with train from Sheffield.
*Photo by Douglas Doherty.*

In due course their train is pulled away from the platform to some temporary resting place clear of the traffic and the Sheffield engine is released to shunt into the engine siding.

There the enginemen fill the tender-tank, run the engine onto the turntable to set it for chimney first running on the return journey, perhaps empty the ashpan and perhaps clean the fire. Then they can take it easy in the enginemen's room where it is warmer especially near the fire, make some tea and eat some food. Most jobs had a fair amount of 'turn-round' time and in many cases the enginemen could find more comfortable resting places than their own footplate.

The Sheffield men might next take a train over Peak Forest to Derby and, after another rest, get back home with a train via Chesterfield. Engine workings on passenger trains tended to remain unchanged for years. Some were more tiresome than others, all tended to become monotonous, and stopping at all stations for long distances depressed enginemen as much as it depressed passengers. But all of them brought a man home pretty fatigued and not entirely clean no matter how much use he had made of the hot water available on every engine.

Equally depressing to everybody was the large amount of time spent by goods trains standing in sidings whilst awaiting a gap in a succession of fast passenger trains. In England the Midland was the first to apply centralised control of movements of goods trains and this substantially reduced idle time of goods engines. Even so the working of goods trains could never be so closely controlled as was necessary for passenger trains if continued patronage were to be ensured and so goods engine men could never say exactly when they would be back home. Some men didn't like this but some didn't mind; it depended on whether you thought that the extra time was worth the extra pay and whether extra time on the railway interfered with other activities that might make money.

Some enginemen found in their jobs a sense of freedom in that, once on a journey there was no-one 'breathing down their necks' except indeed insofar as the driver might do this to his fireman. It was not like working in any one place under the eye of a foreman who could 'sack' any of his men, if he did not like the shape of his face or his manner.

Every railway servant was required to comply with a 'book of rules' developed over the years to tell those responsible for movement of trains exactly what they must do in any set of circumstances that had been experienced or had been imagined to be likely to arise. But the exact mode of handling an engine in conformity with the rules was left to the discretion of the driver and therefore left some scope for individuality. In practice every driver came quickly or slowly to what had been established as good, and probably the best, way of doing anything and so there were no extensive differences between the detail practices of different enginemen.

But however standardised the movements of trains might become it had little influence on the personalities of individual enginemen, on their intelligence or on their personal habits. Some looked spruce and smart throughout each turn of duty. Some started spruce and smart but ended looking rather dirty. They were hardly to be criticised on that account as it was hard to keep clean where about a ton of coal was being shovelled every hour and where draughts were continually spreading coal dust.

The spare-time activities of enginemen were as varied as those of any other group of workers in the same income class. Some enginemen were regular church-goers, and some churchwardens. Some applied themselves to civic interests so far as to become aldermen or mayors. Some were handy about the house, some made models of all sorts of things, some made violins, some repaired washing-machines. Many were satisfied that they had a regular job for life and having gained the measure of it, decided that having worked on the job during the day, they would do no more work on getting home. Some were total abstainers from alcohol while some very bad cases were discharged for being drunk on duty. Smoking was a pastime less easily detected and so there were many infringements of the rule that forbade it.

The profession of engine driving commanded a little more respect than did manual wage-earning in general. Passenger trains were by far the fastest vehicles accessible to the public and this was bound to suggest that the men entrusted with running them were a bit out of the ordinary.

One can well imagine however that anyone who remained in his own town for year after year except for an annual week's holiday might feel some slight awe of a man who went to London and back every day.

*Top:* Gresley P2, 2001 'Cock o' the North'.
*Photo by British Railways, Eastern Region.*

*Bottom:* 60501 'Cock o' the North' as re-built to a Pacific.
*Photo by British Railways, Eastern Region.*

49

Stanier 4–6–2 46251 'City of Nottingham' on Rail Tour duty. On Swindon MPD 9/5/64. *Photo by W. Potter.*

Stanier 'Patriot' 5512 'Bunsen' on Longsight MPD, August 1935. *Photo by W. Potter.*

Stanier 4–6–2 6203 'Princess Margaret Rose' at Edge Hill 1939. *Photo by W. Potter.*

Re-built Stanier 'Patriot' 45514 'Holyhead' draws into Sheffield Midland with the down 'The Thames-Clyde Express'.
*Photo by Douglas Doherty.*

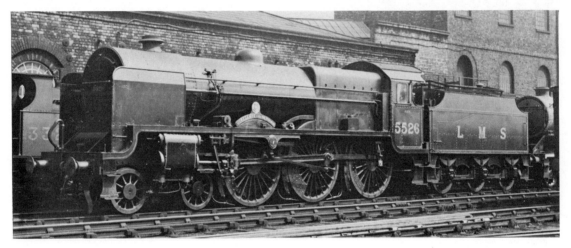

Stanier 'Patriot' 5526 'Morecombe and Heysham'.
*Photo by W. Potter.*

Shortly before 10.00 a.m. at Glasgow Central, Stanier 4–6–2s head southbound trains. On the left is 46221 'Queen Elizabeth' on Birmingham express. On the right is 46220 'Coronation' on the up 'Royal Scot'.
*Photo by Douglas Doherty.*

Stanier re-built 'Scot' 6147 'The Northamptonshire Regiment'.
*Photo by W. Potter.*

Up 'The Mid-day Scot' taking water at Carlisle in 1956. Engine is Stainer 4–6–2 46251 'City of Nottingham'.
*Photo by London Midland Region (B.R.)*

Giving a helping push to a Manchester express out of St. Pancras, is Stanier 2–6–4T 42588.
*Photo by Douglas Doherty.*

On a damp day in April 1939. L,N,E,R, number 10000 at
Doncaster MPD.
*Photo by W. Potter.*

Class W1 4–6–4 number 10000 of the LNER at Doncaster
MPD in April 1939.
*Photo by W. Potter.*

View at King's Cross MPD 29/9/62. On shed are A4s
60032 'Gannet' and 60028 'Walter K. Whigham'.
*Photo by W. Potter.*

# The Story of
# 4472 'Flying Scotsman'

THIS engine was the third of a very distinguished class of British locomotives known as Gresley 'Pacifics'. It was introduced in 1922 on the Great Northern Railway by H. N. Gresley, the Chief Mechanical Engineer, and two such engines, Nos 1470 and 1471 were built in that year. Although it was not the practice of the Great Northern Railway to give names to engines, No. 1470 appeared with the name 'Great Northern' because it was known that a merger of British Railways was impending and that the Great Northern Railway was probably soon to lose its separate identity.

The third engine of the class, No 1472, was not completed till February 1923 by which time the Great Northern Railway had been merged in the London & North Eastern Railway. The engine was given the name 'Flying Scotsman', an unofficial title popularly associated with a train that had left London daily at 10 a.m. for Scotland since about 1860. The engine 'Flying Scotsman' was the first Gresley 'Pacific' to be completed as an LNER locomotive and its number was changed to 4472 in the numbering scheme adopted by that railway.

Like many other engines of the Great Northern Railway, the height of 'Flying Scotsman' was

A close-up of the L.N.E.R. coat of arms carried on the cab-side of 4472.
*Photo by Douglas Doherty.*

reduced to enable it to run on other railways that formed part of the LNER group. This was done by fitting a smaller chimney and dome, and altering the roof of the cab. This brought the engine into its present form apart from not readily noticeable changes in details over the years.

The tender attached to the preserved engine is not quite like the original one, on which the top part of the coal supply was retained by horizontal rails instead of the continuous steel wall now used.

The second tender that at present accompanies the preserved engine and tender was never used in actual service. It has been added solely as an extra water-tank, because with the scrapping of steam locomotives on British Railways the water supplies required by such locomotives have nearly all been scrapped. No steam engine can now run very far on British Railways unless it has with it much more water than used to suffice.

Long non-stop runs could be made without very big tenders because water was picked up on the fly from track-pans. For many years Gresley 'Pacifics' like 'Flying Scotsman' ran regular

A close-up, of 4472's left hand
nameplate.
*Photo by Douglas Doherty.*

*Bottom left (opposite page):*
On the footplate. Whilst the driver
concentrates upon the road ahead, the
fireman stokes the ever hungry furnace
with coal. Note the very narrow hole
through which the fireman has to guide
each shovelful of coal.
*Photo by British Railways.*

trains non-stop between London and Edinburgh, 393 miles. ( The longest non-stop run ever made by a steam locomotive was over the 438 miles from Jersey City to Pittsburgh on a very special occasion in 1876) Only in Great Britain was there ever a regular non-stop run over any distance longer than about 220 miles.

The regular LNER run of 393 miles was practicable only by use of a special tender through which enginemen could pass from the train to the engine in order to run it over the second half of the journey whilst the first men rode in the train.

'Flying Scotsman', like all Gresley 'Pacifics' has three cylinders. This feature, not uncommon in Great Britain, has been used in only very few American locomotives. The third cylinder in 'Flying Scotsman' is under the smokebox and it is very difficult, however close you get to the engine, to see anything of it. The valve that lets steam into it and out of it is worked through a special mechanism by the front ends of the spindles of the valves over the outside cylinders.

The Gresley 'Pacifics' were among the finest British locomotives and they distinguished themselves in many ways. 'Flying Scotsman' herself was one of the engines that made the two 393-mile non-stops on the first day of the regular service in 1928. In the course of two very fast experimental runs made non-stop between London and Leeds (186 miles) in 1934 she became the second British locomotive to be reliably timed at 100 m.p.h.

In 1938 a Gresley 'Pacific' of Class A4, which was a modified form of the original Gresley 'Pacific' with streamlined covering, reached in a special test the top speed of 126 m.p.h. which is the world's record for steam locomotives. In regular service with streamlined trains, although nominally limited to 90 m.p.h., Class A4 engines reached 100 m.p.h. from time to time. The same engines were also used for heavier trains and could average a mile a minute over hundreds of miles with trains weighing up to 600 tons.

To pull 600 tons on the level at 60 m.p.h. the fire has to burn a pound of coal every second and this made hard work for the fireman when sustained over several hours. He did not need to work non-stop; in many parts of an average journey made by a Gresley 'Pacific' the fireman might shovel 200 pounds of coal onto the fire in the course of a minute or so and then rest for two or three minutes, but it was hard work nevertheless.

Perhaps the most difficult job was to run between London and Newcastle with three intermediate stops and a running average of nearly 60 m.p.h. In the ordinary way the load was not more than 500 tons but occasionally it could be 600 tons and the schedule still applied, without any helper-engine. Many drivers would fire the engine for stretches of 20 miles or so to give the fireman a rest on the long hard jobs, but this was not an official practice as the driver is responsible for the safety of the train. So a fireman could have a rest of this kind only if the driver could trust him to watch where they were going and to interpret every signal correctly.

The most important job on the engine itself was to make sure that there was enough water in the boiler. If the water level in the gauge glass dropped

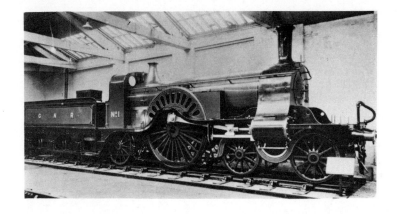

Great-grandfather to 4472 was this 'Single-Wheeler', built at the Doncaster Works of the Great Northern Railway, (G.N.R.) in 1870 to the designs of Patrick Stirling, the G.N.R. locomotive engineer. No. 1 hauled the 'Scotch Expresses' for many years, and participated in the inter-route 'races' from London to Aberdeen in 1888.
*Photo by British Railways.*

The 'Singles' eventually had to give way to larger and more powerful locomotives developed from them. On the new engines, the larger and heavier boilers required more wheels in the chassis to support them. Here is shown Britain's first 'Atlantic' (pioneered in the U.S.A.) or 4–4–2 wheeled engine, No. 990. Designed by H. A. Ivatt, the successor to Stirling on the G.N.R., and built at Doncaster Works in 1898. No. 990 was named 'Henry Oakley' after the Chairman of the G.N.R.

*Photo by British Railways.*

A '251' in L.N.E.R. days, leaving King's-Cross with a 'Scotch Express'. Note the 'Somersault' type signals inherited from the G.N.R. On the 'Scotch Expresses' the engines were changed at Grantham and then at York, where an ex-North Eastern Railway (N.E.R.), loco would take over for the onward journey to Newcastle. The old G.N.R., made an end-on connection with the N.E.R. just north of Doncaster.
*Photo by F. R. Hebron.*

*Bottom left (opposite page):*
A 'Klondyke' racing along the L.N.E.R. main line over a set of water track-pans. The pick-up scoop is lowered before reaching the water-pans. When the track-pan is reached the rail line descends a few inches in elevation, so lowering the loco and the scoop dips into the pan and tender filling commences. The reverse procedure happens at the end of the track-pan length, although the scoop will probably have been lifted out before then as the tender water tank is filled rapidly.
*Photo by F. R. Hebron.*

As the 'Scotch Expresses' became heavier, a corresponding increase in size of motive power took place. The 'Klondykes' gave way to the '251' class of 'Atlantics', built to the designs of H. A. Ivatt from 1902 onwards. A larger boiler was placed on a chassis similar to the one on the 'Klondykes', but a close inspection of the boiler fire-box ends of 251 and 990 will reveal a significant difference. The fire-box on 990 slots inside the main-frames. On 251 the fire-box rests on top of the main-frames, this design permitting a very wide fire-box to cope with the very high steam rates used in hauling heavy, sustained high speed trains. We now see 4472 taking shape. No. 251 is preserved at York.
*Photo by British Railways.*

In 1911, Herbert Nigel Gresley, (left on the picture) succeeded Ivatt as Locomotive Carriage and Wagon Superintendant of the G.N.R. 11 years after taking office, Gresley's first 'Pacific' type 4–6–2 appeared from Doncaster Works, designed to combat the ever growing demands of heavier and faster trains. 4472 was the 3rd 'Pacific' Gresley built, and its development can be traced from the '251s'.
*Photo by C. Smith.*

4472, hauling the celebrated 'Flying Scotsman' train (as the 'Scotch Expresses' later became), and makes a fine picture as it thunders through London's suburbs in the 1930s. By now the cab and chimney had been reduced in height in order to permit greater route availability over the L.N.E.R. system.
*Photo by F. R. Hebron.*

The shape of things to come. On trials on the main line where once 4472 reigned supreme is pioneer English Electric 'Deltic' diesel-electric locomotive of 3,300 h.p. The trials proving successful, British Railways ordered 22 of these locomotives for service on the ex-L.N.E.R. main line, replacing the 'Pacifics' as they were withdrawn. 'Deltic', painted pale blue and silver and now preserved is shown here at Retford on a King's Cross to Hull express in April 1960.
*Photo by Douglas Doherty.*

4472 soon after it was built, in King's Cross loco yard. The livery is that which adorned 4472 when it was exhibited in 1924 at the British Empire Exhibition at Wembley. This livery is not the one carried in L.N.E.R. service. Note 4472's original state with high cab, dome and chimney, and coal rail on tender.
*Photo by F. R. Hebron.*

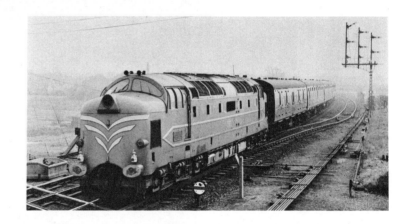

Following Gresley as Chief Mechanical Engineer of the L.N.E.R. was Edward Thompson. Following Thompson was Arthur H. Peppercorn, who continued building 'Pacifics' developed from Gresley's magnificent machines. Shown here at Doncaster is Peppercorn A.1 class 'Pacific' No. 60136 'Alcazar' in June 1961.
*Photo by Douglas Doherty.*

Preserved 4472 wearing its 1965 Darlington Works re-paint, and now confined to working enthusiast's special trains, waits at York to depart southwards to King's Cross with the 'White Rose' tour in May 1965.
*Photo by Keith Pirt.*

4472 featured a much larger boiler than 251, almost up to the limit of the loading gauge, and needed an extra pair of driving wheels to carry it, The wide fire-box used on 251 was retained and enlarged.
*Photo by British Railways.*

out of sight, there was danger that the top of the firebox would become so softened by overheating that the boiler would explode. So every engine-man automatically looked at the gauge-glass as soon as he got into the cab and did it every few minutes so long as he remained there. It was the fireman's duty to keep one (or both) of the two injectors going in such a way as to keep the water level above the danger-limit. This in turn meant that the water supply in the tender had to be enough to take the engine to the next stopping place where there was a water-crane or of course to the next track-pan.

On the East Coast route from London to Scotland the distances between successive track-pans varied between 24 miles and 96 miles. The longest gap was apt to be 'borderline' with a heavy train and a driver might have to limit the engine's effort over that stretch to the capacity of the tender to hold water rather than to the power of the boiler to boil it.

Steam locomotives normally ran very roughly compared with passenger cars. They would roll and sway and bump in a way that can hardly be understood by anyone who has never actually experienced it. When first put into service after building or after general repairs a locomotive might ride well, but wear and tear made matters worse and shortly before each general repair became necessary the riding could be so bad that speed on downgrades might have to be restricted on that account.

Firemen came to learn how to do their work where no ordinary person could stand up without holding on, but even firemen could be beaten by the worst antics of a 'run-down' engine.

In Britain, 'Pacifics' rode better than most other classes of locomotive and the Gresley 'Pacifics' were among the best in this respect. Indeed on the first demonstration run of a streamlined version of the Gresley 'Pacific', some of the more knowledgeable passengers in the train were alarmed by the wild running of the cars at over 100 m.p.h. whereas there was nothing in the running of the locomotive to suggest to the enginemen that the high speed was causing any apprehension.

During World War II there were no very fast runs in Britain, but Gresley 'Pacifics' took very heavy ones at moderate speeds. They struggled along in what eventually became a bad state of disrepair, but when reasonably high standards were eventually re-attained after the war, the Gresley 'Pacifics' again showed that they were of a quality unsurpassed in the world.

# 'Flying Scotsman'
# Fact Check List

Of all the thousands of steam locomotives that have ever run in Great Britain none could be a more worthy representative than 'Flying Scotsman'. Other classes of engine could be named as possible rivals, and differences of opinion on the matter might have been expressed by British railway enthusiasts with strong emotion if there had been occasion to ask for them, but there could be no reason for disapproving the choice.

When it appeared in 1922, this class of locomotive represented a notable advance in British practice and its work for forty years afterwards is a record of reliability all the time and brilliance when required. It holds world records in at least two respects.

'Flying Scotsman' was the third of a class of 52 'Pacifics' built to the designs of H. N. Gresley, Chief Mechanical Engineer of the Great Northern Railway between 1921 and 1926. There had been only one previous British 'Pacific', a four-cylinder engine built by the Great Western Railway in 1908; there was no need on that line for anything so big, and the Great Western built no other 'Pacific'.

Barrow Hill, Stavely near Chesterfield. Preserved 4472 is being coaled for its return journey to London. The occasion was a special train from London to Chesterfield, to visit the Chatsworth estate, a noted Stately Home. The train was called "Michaelangelo Tour" and ran in 1967.
*Photo by Keith Pirt.*

The driver of preserved 4472 watches his progress as he arrives tender first at Sheffield Victoria. The engine is going to the other end of the station to top up with water before joining its train, a Cleethorpes excursion. 9.10 a.m. 27th May 1969.
*Photo by Douglas Doherty.*

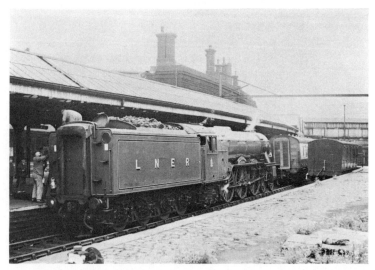

Taking on water before heading out of Sheffield Victoria with a Cleethorpes excursion on 27th May 1969. The tender corridor connection can be clearly seen in this shot. 9.30 a.m.
*Photo by Douglas Doherty.*

10 a.m. in the mid 1930s, and the 'Flying Scotsman' train sets off from King's Cross on its non-stop journey to Edinburgh. Motive power is provided by 'Pacific' No. 2596 'Manna', a sister of 4472.
*Photo by British Railways.*

When the production batch of 'Deltics' appeared, slight external styling had taken place. No. D9003 was only a few weeks old when photographed at Doncaster on a down Hull express on a rainy day in May 1961. Behind is Gresley 'Pacific' No. 60098 'Spion Kop' fresh off a works overhaul and engaged on light duties during 'running in'.
*Photo by Douglas Doherty.*

An 8.15 a.m. shot of preserved 4472 departing from Doncaster with an enthusiast's special for Carlisle and Newcastle. Note 4472's extra tender carrying additional supplies of water for its journey. Doncaster works in background.
*Photo by Douglas Doherty.*

Throwing a fine exhaust preserved 4472 is setting off from Doncaster with a special train of enthusiasts for Carlisle and Newcastle. 8.15 a.m. 1/6/69. *Photo by Douglas Doherty.*

The last lap. Its journey almost at an end "Flying Scotsman" sets off from Doncaster hauling a London-West Riding express. The Locomotive and Carriage and Wagon works can be seen in the background. 10/5/61. 10.42 a.m
*Photo by Douglas Doherty.*

Preserved 4472's first outing sporting its extra tender. The occasion is an excursion form Gainsboro' to Blackpool in 1967. The loco and train seen here approaching Copy Pit, Lancashire.
*Picture by Keith Pirt.*

*Left:*
4472 at the start of its journey northwards from King's Cross. A very unusual view. The engine's nose will shortly veer left to follow the rail track seen immediately above her chimney, and guide her into the tunnel.
*Photo by British Railways.*

*Bottom:*
Preserved 4472 pauses in Dalmeny sidings during a lull in her posings for her Cuneo painting in May 1964.
*Photo by Keith Pirt.*

*Top (opposite page):*
York shed, May 1967. Preserved 4472 receives beauty treatment at the hands of willing volunteers. 4472 had worked the "Cathedrals Express" from Norwich to York and is idling her time until due to return later.
*Photo by Keith Pirt.*

*Bottom (opposite page):*
In May 1964, preserved 4472 was the subject of a painting by Terence Cuneo, whose composition showed 4472 hauling a train across the Forth Bridge in Scotland. 4472 made a number of journeys back and forth for the benefit of the artist. Here 4472 is backing off the Bridge into Dalmeny station after a session of posing.
*Photo by Keith Pirt.*

The up "The White Rose" express passing Doncaster Central Goods Depot. This titled express connects Leeds with London. Doncaster Central station can be seen in the left background. The stationary locomotive behind is the "standby", and is Peppercorn designed A1 class Pacific No. 60126 "Sir Vincent Raven". 4472 is shown in British Railways days when numbered 60103. 4.50 p.m. 13/5/61.
*Photo by Douglas Doherty.*

On some British railways, all the big passenger train engines had individual names. On the Great Northern Railway that was not the case although one locomotive, the first Great Northern 'Atlantic' was given the name of 'Henry Oakley' the General Manager who had just retired from that position in 1898.

The first Great Northern 'Pacific' was given the name 'Great Northern' because within a year the Great Northern Railway itself was going to 'retire' by being merged with other railways. The second 'Pacific' was named, 'Sir Frederick Banbury', after the last Chairman of the Great Northern Railway.

The name, 'Flying Scotsman', of the third 'Pacific' was one that had been popularly associated (without any official recognition) with a London–Scotland train that had left King's Cross Station in London for Edinburgh at 10 a.m. on every weekday since about 1862, The adjective 'flying' arose from the impression that Great Northern trains to Scotland ran very fast. There was justification for this in that for some years in the nineteenth century the Great Northern were running the fastest regular trains in the world. But for a large part of its later career the Great Northern train known as 'Flying Scotsman' did not in fact have a very fast time-card.

'Flying Scotsman' was the second British locomotive to be reliably timed at 100 m.p.h. She reached this speed in running down a half per cent grade during the course of a special high-speed test-run in November 1934. What was more striking at the time, however, was that, earlier in the same day, she had run *up* that grade at about 82 m.p.h.

'Flying Scotsman' was the first locomotive to run a regular train without a stop over the 393 miles between London and Edinburgh. This was on the first day of May in 1928. A train started from each end of the course at 10 a.m. and was scheduled to arrive at 6.15 p.m. The train from Edinburgh reached London at 6.12 p.m. but as 'Flying Scotsman' had taken the north-bound train into Edinburgh at 6.3 p.m. she was the first to complete the non-stop journey.

This non-stop run was made in each direction five days a week during the summers of 1928 to 1939. It was, by a long way, the world's record long run by a train in regular service. (The world record of 438 miles was made once in special circumstances on the Pennsylvania R.R. in 1876).

Access to the locomotive from the train was afforded by a passage through a specially-built tender and so the men who would run the engine over the second half of the journey rode in the train for the first half.

'Flying Scotsman' has three cylinders, two of them in the usual positions, and a third under the smokebox where it is hidden from the ordinary onlooker. He may, however, notice that, when running, the engine gives six exhaust beats during every revolution of the driving wheels and he may get the false impression that three cylinders give an engine phenomenal acceleration. That is not so; the main advantage from three cylinders is reduction of hammer-blow on the track and reduction of vibration in the locomotive.

Three-cylinder steam locomotives were always rare in America whereas when the railways of Britain were nationalised in 1948 their 20,000 locomotives included over 1900 of the three-cylinder type. Of these, over 1000 belonged to the London & North Eastern Railway into which the Great Northern Railway had been merged at the beginning of 1923. About 300 British locomotives had four cylinders but over 88 per cent of the total stock were of the usual 2-cylinder types.

The connecting rods and side rods on 'Flying Scotsman' are very much thinner and lighter than those to be seen on locomotives of comparable size. They are in fact light even by British standards and this has been made possible by using alloy steel very carefully machined and heat-treated to make the steel as strong as it can

This side view showing nameplate of "Flying Scotsman" also shows the connecting rods—thinner and lighter as becomes a thoroughbred—of special alloy steel and heat treated.
*Photo by Douglas Doherty.*

Forging ahead through Scot's country-side near Milathort, preserved 4472 heads an Edinburgh-Aberdeen special via Perth in May 1964
*Photo by Keith Pirt*

With steam shut off "Flying Scotsman" coasts into the platform at Retford for its service stop. Retford is situated just south of Doncaster and is an interchange point for traffic in the East/West direction. 11.10 a.m. 30/4/60. Note the double chimney conversion.
*Photo by Douglas Doherty.*

A lovely portrait of preserved 4472, taken when on Basingstoke shed in September 1966. Our hero had worked up the "Farnborough Flier" from the North Country.
*Photo by Keith Pirt.*

be. Although some engineers would prefer to see rods a little huskier than these, they have worked well during many years of hard work.

The second tender behind 'Flying Scotsman' during her infrequent tours is simply a water tank. It has been used in Great Britain only since the general abandonment of the steam locomotive and the consequent removal of most of the means of supplying water to steam engines on the railway.

Most of the Gresley 'Pacifics' built after 'Flying Scotsman' were named after successful race-horses. The first of them, No. 4473 'Solario' made some British railway history by running a train of eleven coaches over 140 miles at an average of 74 m.p.h.

Gresley 'Pacifics', after the first lot of 52, were built with boilers designed for steam at 220 p.s.i. (instead of the original 180 p.s.i.) and 'Flying Scotsman' now has one such boiler.

From 1935 Gresley 'Pacifics' were fitted with boilers for 250 p.s.i. and with a streamlined casing. One such locomotive ('Mallard', No. 4468) reached the world's record speed for steam locomotives of 126 m.p.h. during a special test in July 1938. In ordinary service this A4 Class of 'Pacific' averaged 75 m.p.h. over long distances with 320-ton trains or 60 m.p.h. with 600-ton trains.

The Gresley 'Pacifics' worked all the heaviest and fastest passenger trains over London & North Eastern Railway for over twenty years. Larger 'Pacifics' were built after World War II to share their work but, even with all allowance for the less favourable operating conditions than those between the wars, the highest standard of performance of the Gresley 'Pacifics' was never surpassed.

'Flying Scotsman' is fired with coal by hand. In the ordinary way no fireman's job in Great Britain was so hard as was the heaviest manual work required on say American locomotives and no mechanical stoker was used, other than experimentally, on any British locomotive.

In its provision for comfort of the enginemen, the cab on 'Flying Scotsman' is one of the best ever to be used in Great Britain. It is not so spacious as the average American cab. This is partly because the width has to be more closely restricted and partly because no provision is made to accommodate more than two men at once. A third man would ride on an engine occasionally to investigate complaints about it or about its riding over particular stretches of track but he had to use what space the enginemen left clear for him.

Members of the general public on boarding a locomotive are apt to think that enginemen behind a big boiler cannot properly see where they are going. In Great Britain, where all tracks are carefully fenced against the general public, the enginemen need not normally see anything but the signals and this can be done, if necessary, through a very small area of front window. For its size the Gresley 'Pacific' is one of the best British engines in this respect.

Because railways in Britain are thoroughly fenced and all level crossings with roads are (or were till recently) provided with gates and officials to work them, nothing but trains can occupy the tracks and it is unnecessary to provide any locomotive with a strong head light. After dark the driver works entirely by signal lights and confidently runs at full speed in complete darkness. (Some of the fastest British trains run for most of the year in darkness). The locomotive does, however, carry small headlights (steam locomotives normally had oil-lamps) arranged in a pattern to indicate the class of train and of course to give some warning to anyone who needed to be on the track after dark. But even if the oil headlights went out, the train was not stopped on that account. On the other hand, any train that passed a signal-box with no visible tail-light was stopped at the next signal box to have the matter put right.

So any powerful headlamp you may see on 'Flying Scotsman' is there purely for use in America.

Every engine had four lamp-brackets at the front and lamps, easily movable by hand, were set in the right brackets for the class of train even in daylight. On some railways, the lamps were painted white so as to be more readily visible in daylight by signalmen and others who could use the information given by their positions.

No steam locomotive remains in service on British Railways and it is only by the enterprise and enthusiasm of Mr. A. F. Pegler that 'Flying Scotsman' is kept in a condition to run trains over long distances. For this, all those with interest in railways and locomotives will always gratefully admire his devotion to the task of keeping 'Flying Scotsman' fit to fly.

The following figures relate to 'Flying Scotsman' fully loaded with coal and water.

| | |
|---|---|
| Maximum diameter of boiler | 77 in |
| Length of tubes | 228 in |
| Grate area | 41.25 sq. ft. |
| Working pressure of steam | 220 p.s.i. |
| Total evaporative heating surface | 2692 sq. ft. |
| Diameter and stroke of pistons | 19 × 26 in. |
| Diameter of piston valves | 8 in. |
| Diameter of driving wheels | 80 in. |
| Weight on driving wheels | 150000 pounds |
| Total weight of locomotive | 216000 ,, |
| Coal capacity of tender | 18000 ,, |
| Water capacity of tender | 5000 gallons |
| Total weight of tender | 130000 pounds |
| Nom. tractive effort at 85% boiler pressure | 32,909 lbs. |

Preserved 4472 in Doncaster works yard fresh off her pre October 1969 tour of U.S.A. overhaul and paint job. A number of special items are fitted to comply with regulations in the States, Cow-catcher, buckeye coupling and headlamp among them. The lamp has not yet been fitted at this stage. The bell was presented to 4472 by the Southern Railway System of U.D.A. Farewell for now 4472, we look forward to your triumphal return.
*Photo by Doncaster Newspapers Ltd.*

Gresley's mixed traffic masterpiece, 4771 'Green Arrow'. *Photo by British Railways, Eastern Region.*

'Castle' class 5012 'Berry Pomeroy Castle' hauling the Birkenhead-Bournemouth through train near Knowle and Dorridge. 27/12/60. *Photo by Michael Mensing.*

# "Quotes"

*These quotations have been culled from the pages of* **Model Railway News** *and appeared in the years from its foundation in 1925 to just after the outbreak of war. Some seem strangely 'period' to us today; other could have been written in any model magazine only last month!*

## JANUARY 1925

How many model railway clubs are there in this country? We only know of three—the Model Railway Club of London, the Wimbledon Model Railway Club, and the new club at Mill Hill School.

## JANUARY 1926

Making No. 'OO' gauge track is a proposition which has got to be solved. There are already many brains actively engaged on the problem and we will, of course, publish notes of any attempt to produce a type of home-made track that we hear of.

## SEPTEMBER 1927

A new name for $3\frac{1}{2}$ mm. gauge (sic) is coming into use in some corners of the model railway world. This is 'HO' gauge, which means half 'O' gauge to distinguish it from the 4 mm. scale which is adopted in the trade for 'OO' gauge. It is a convenient way of making a distinction which is certainly necessary in view of the fact that each scale has its own confirmed adherents.

## NOVEMBER 1928

Who makes the ridiculous contraptions that are to be found at various places of amusement and on seaside piers, labelled 'working model railway'? We all see them at some place or other, smile at them and pass by. There is usually a circular length of tinplate rail, a tunnel, a bridge, a windmill, an enchanted castle, some gigantic cows and sheep, a crude shed and stumpy platform representing a station, and a toy engine with the colours of one group and the name of another, but resembling neither. A few signals planted about in the wrong places, and rocks and trees and houses, of the crudest possible kind, complete the model—or rather, the 'muddle'. One day somebody will make a really decent working model railway, with a coin-actuated mechanism, and the pennies will be dropping in all day long. The attraction of any good working model is irresistible to most people, and a model railway is perhaps the most attractive of all.

## AUGUST 1929

Buffer locking can be mitigated and closer coupling of coaches made possible by only fixing buffers to the one end of coaches. The same method is used in actual practice on the permanently coupled sets of suburban coaches.

## FEBRUARY 1930

We have lately seen a very real novelty in 'OO' gauge locomotives, a real working steam model in that miniature gauge. This is not yet on the market, but it has been built by an enthusiast who has developed the design to a really successful stage. He is anxious to dispose of the design and experimental experience to a manufacturing firm, who will put the engine into production. If any our readers are interested we shall be pleased to forward correspondence to the designer. We imagine very few 'OO' gauge owners have dreamed of a steam locomotive for their service. It now seems to be a really practical possibility.

## SEPTEMBER 1931

Model railway enthusiasts are to be found in all walks of life, and it is therefore not surprising to learn that the well-known comedian, Mr. Jack Hulbert, has a miniature railway in his garden at his home in Curzon Street. In view of his interest in railway matters, it was appropriate that Jack Hulbert should have played a prominent part in the 'talkie' of that successful play, 'The Ghost Train'. Model trains were used in securing some of the effects in this film. The late George Grossmith was another theatrical celebrity who delighted to amuse himself with model locomotives as a recreation from his arduous stage work.

## JANUARY 1932

In the real railway world 1932 will be a year of progress. Recent experiments indicate that considerable attention is being given both to faster running, and to longer non-stop runs.

There is no doubt that the railway companies are fully alive to the seriousness of the competition from other means of transport with which they are confronted, and are leaving no stone unturned to improve their own services along logical and well-considered lines. While a railway may be at a disadvantage in some respects compared with road transport, it has certain very definite advantages peculiarly its own. It has a right of way on a clear and direct road, it has no restrictive speed limit, it is not subject to 'traffic jams', there is no 'cutting in' on the road, there is no risk through incompetent or inexperienced drivers, there is no stoppage for meals on long runs, and there is a maximum of cleanliness and comfort for the passenger. Moreover, the safety of the railway is at a remarkably high level. It is more than likely that improved railway service will win back a lot of passengers who have temporarily forsaken it for the adventures of the open road.

## JUNE 1933

A model railway should not be a dumb show. It should be used, and used to transport model people and miniature commodities. By this we do not mean that model passengers should be made to hop in and out of carriages, but the coaches, horse boxes, milk vans and other vehicles common to express, ordinary and local trains should be employed. Such as are detached and attached in the working time-table should be arranged to be dealt with in the proper manner. The working out of coach movements and providing engines at the right time and place to work trains is a task which requires some skill. It is well known that model clockwork locomotives are favoured by many readers, and although we are always hopeful that continued improvements will be made in mechanisms, so long as enough engines are available, the necessary winding-up is not a troublesome matter. A terminal-to-terminal line suits them best. Goods trains should be employed to move goods and the evolutions of wagons necessary to the transport of the goods in a likely manner, will provide a good deal of instructive amusement and require some skill.

Camden MPD and 46108 'Seaforth Highlander' on turntable after having brought up a boat special from Liverpool. 25/8/59. *Photo by Douglas Doherty.*

## OCTOBER 1934

A correspondent relates that he recently had occasion to enter a store where a special display of model aeroplanes was being made. On talking to those in charge of the exhibit, he mentioned that his own hobby was model railway work. He was promptly told "Model railways are dying out, there is not much doing with them nowadays, aeroplanes are all the rage." A walk round the recent 'M.E.' exhibition, or visit to any model railway club meeting would provide an effective answer. The fact that one hobby happens to be growing is no proof that another hobby is dead. To argue that way is simply a confession of ignorance, and may be regarded accordingly.

## JANUARY 1937

### SCALE OR GAUGE

The large amount of correspondence, which has come to us during recent months, on the subject of 'scale v. standard,' has revealed that there is still a marked tendency to mix up the terms 'HO' and 'OO'. This confusion of terms is unfortunate, because its effect is to lead to quite unnecessary misunderstanding as between traders and their customers, causing much correspondence which could otherwise be avoided. In an effort to elucidate the matter we would point out that the term 'HO' applies to $3\frac{1}{2}$ mm. scale models, built to run on 16.5 mm. gauge track; the term 'OO' applies to 4 mm. scale models built to run on 19 mm. gauge track. These dimensions are standard, and are generally accepted by the trade. But, unfortunately, there are many 4 mm. scale models built to run on 16.5 mm. gauge; and to these the term 'OO' is usually applied—presumably, because the models are 4 mm. *scale*!—and this is where the confusion arises. We know of no term applying to this mix-up of scale and gauge; neither do we wish, at the moment, to discuss the rights and wrongs of mixing the two in this manner. We attach no blame to traders who cater for the 'mongrel' arrangement; but we suggest that, in future, it should not be designated 'OO'. As we have said, the term 'OO' gauge applies to 19 mm., or $\frac{3}{4}''$ gauge-track, for which the correct scale is 4 mm. to the foot. We hope that the unfortunate mixture of the two will eventually disappear from our ken. Our American friends quickly stamped it out, before it obtained too great a hold; and, today,

they refuse to countenance it. To them, and to enthusiasts in other parts of the world, the terms 'HO' and 'OO' mean precisely what we have stated above, and nothing else. It is high time that we, in this country, followed suit, so as to avoid any further misunderstanding in the matter.

## JANUARY 1938

### THE CRITIC

At the recent 'M.E.' Exhibition, a model S.R. 2-6-0, in course of construction, was to be seen on one of the Club stands. The seven-year-old daughter of a gentleman whose name is not unknown to our readers, studied the model, then read the label on which the model was described as a 'U' class engine. There came a burst of childish laughter, followed by the decidedly audible remark, heard by everyone in the vicinity, "That's not a 'U' it's an 'N'!" She was right! If the younger generation is becoming as sharp-eyed as this, then we older locomotive enthusiasts really must be more careful.

## APRIL 1940

### NOT WHAT IT SEEMS

In an article published in a recent issue of our American contemporary, *The Model Railroader*, there occurs the following sentence: "Before you paint the model run it enough to iron out the bugs so you get a smoothly running job. Mind you, there will be bugs; there are in every engine, so don't be discouraged if you find a few." To English readers, this sentence come upon for the first time, is apt to be disconcerting, not to say puzzling, since the particularly unpleasant entomological specimens referred to are no more likely to be found in a model than they are anywhere else in the workshop! But the sentence does not mean exactly what it seems to suggest in literal terms; actually, the advice given is absolutely sound and thoroughly sensible. Translated into everyday English, it means that a model should be properly run-in before it is painted, so that the stiffness, inherent in a new model, can be eliminated. The stiffness is almost invariably due to high spots in gears and bearing surfaces, and is found in new mechanisms of all kinds, but particularly in small model locomotives. Builders of the latter, therefore, should not feel disgruntled if, on the first trial, their locomotives do not run as freely as was expected.

# A Snowplough for 009

## by Michael Andress

THIS small snowplough is a quick and easy model to make and it will add a little variety to the scene on your line. Even if you don't want to sprinkle your layout with flour, salt, plaster, or what have you to simulate a snow scene, this vehicle can be left on a siding by your engine shed. My model is loosely based on the standard gauge wagon-mounted plough shown in Photos 6 and 7 on page 79.

I used the Eggerbahn small goods wagon as the basis of this model, but I think production of this wagon has been discontinued, though a few may still be available secondhand. Alternatively, the larger and still marketed Playcraft/Eggerbahn Dropside Goods Wagon (P25) could be used.

The plough itself was built up from 10 and 20 thou. thick plastic card. The back, top, bottom, centre, and intermediate pieces were cut from 20 thou. thick plastic card to the patterns shown full size in Fig. 1. If you plan to leave the coupling on the front end of the wagon, parts of the back, centre and intermediate pieces should be cut away before assembly so that the plough will fit over the coupling. Alternatively, if the plough is to be fixed permanently to the wagon you can remove the coupling and in this case there is no need to cut away any parts of the plough pieces. The parts are then cemented together using Mek Pak solvent, fitting the top and bottom pieces to the front of the plough back level with the top and bottom edges respectively. The centre piece is also fitted to the back between the top and bottom

and the two intermediate pieces can then be fixed in place. Make sure that all parts are fitted square and true and then allow to set hard. The two curved faces of the plough were cut from 10 thou. thick plastic card, each being cut so that it was slightly oversize. I fitted one of these in place and held it until the cement fixed it in position, then trimmed it to exact size with a sharp knife and a fine file before similarly fitting the other curved plate. This was also cut down to exact size and final finishing was with a fine file and sandpaper after filling in any small gaps with body filler. I then painted the plough (red oxide) and mounted it on the front of the wagon.

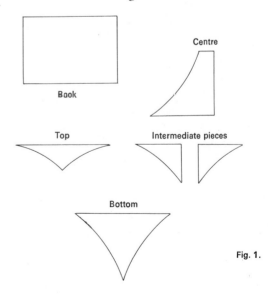

Fig. 1.

# Snowploughs

## by Michael Andress

1

NOW that winter, with its leaden skies and falls of snow, is here again it seems an opportune moment to look at some snowploughs. Widely used in America and Europe they are less often needed in Britain, but a variety of types are and have been used here. The examples shown here include both standard and narrow gauge types.

The simplest form of all is the pilot plough fixed either temporarily or permanently to the front, or front and rear, of a steam, diesel or electric locomotive.

*Photo* 1. This simple wedge shaped plough is mounted on a Swedish Railways Z4p class diesel engine (891 mm gauge). The locomotive was photographed on dual gauge trackage at Västervik.

2

5

4

3

6

9

7

10

8

*Photo* 2. Another simple arrangement. Two curved plates fitted one to each side of Vira, a 60 cm gauge preserved locomotive running on the Ö.S.J. at Mariefred, Sweden. Note the superb headlights.

*Photo* 3. Similar plates on an Rb3 class Swedish Railways electric locomotive pictured leaving Uppsala station.

*Photo* 4. Plates of this type are sometimes fitted to British Rail diesels. This example was photographed recently at Gateshead motive power depot. (English Electric Class 37 diesel-electric No. 6913).

*Photo* 5. Wedge ploughs are also used on road vehicles and I've included this picture because I think it would make an interesting and unusual addition to the lineside scene on a model railway layout.

The second group of snowploughs is the type in which the plough is mounted on a wagon, either an old goods wagon or locomotive tender or one especially built to carry a simple plough.

*Photos* 6 *and* 7. Two views of a British wagon mounted snowplough photographed at Consett in County Durham. This vehicle is the one on which my 009 model is based.

*Photos* 8 *and* 9. Two similar tender ploughs, one a four-wheeler and the other a six-wheeler, photographed at Ystad in Southern Sweden. Note the light mounted on the top of each plough.

*Photos* 10 *and* 11. Two views of two Danish Railway snowploughs at Copenhagen. The larger eight-wheel vehicle is rather similar to the two Swedish ploughs. The other appears to be largely of wooden construction with an elaborately

11

12

13

14

shaped curved ploughing surface, which is incorporated into the body of the vehicle.

The third group are the more elaborate specially built snowploughs with a cabin in which a railwayman can ride. Often he can raise or lower, or otherwise adjust the plough as necessary.

*Photo* 12. About the simplest form possible of this type is this narrow gauge snowplough awaiting restoration at Mariefred, Sweden. A model of this plough is a future addition to my 009 rolling stock roster.

*Photos* 13 *and* 14. Two views of British Rail snowplough No. 986, one of several identical vehicles based at Gateshead.

*Photo* 15. This Roslagen Railway 891 mm gauge snowplough has an adjustable plough with wing blades which can be swung out when the vehicle is in use. Photographed at Rimbo, 34 miles north of Stockholm.

*Photo* 16. A similar standard gauge plough used by Swedish Railways.

*Photo* 17. A large West German bogie snowplough at Hameln.

*Photo* 18. This Swedish vehicle has small adjustable blades at front and back which could be used for clearing small falls of snow from the track. Note also the flanger blade beneath the cabin to clear each side of the running rails.

16

15

17

18

'County' class 4–6–0 on Chester MPD.
*Photo by Douglas Doherty.*

Thompson's light mixed traffic loco for the LNER, 900 class
**L1**. *Photo by British Railways, Eastern Region.*

# Up the Garden Path

## by Alex Bowie

ALTHOUGH a 4 mm. user, I believe that the big gauges are far more satisfactory outdoors. One cannot scale garden worms or dirt, and the big L.G.B. trains have a much better chance of coping with these and other hazards. Besides which, I rather fancy that these very quaint, and not so small, slim gauge trains will look more at home among the miniature plants than even the more usual 'O' gauge.

The L.G.B. trains, because they are 'off the shelf' and almost irresistably attractive, will probably appeal to people who would not previously even have considered outdoor railways. Because of this, I think I should repeat the experts' warning about electrical gear used outdoors. This must be installed with more than average care, and on no account should very ancient or hastily improvised equipment be used.

Personally, if I were a family man lucky enough to have the space and cash (and enthusiastic helpers) I would build a shed for the terminal and main controls at each end of the line, with plenty of glass so that the main line of the railway could be clearly seen. Alternatively, one room at the back of the house, or part of a garage, could be used at one end, with a shed at the other. However, although these things are ideal, we have to face up to the fact that most of us would be lucky even to have one room or shed, and usually there must be a compromise. With this in mind, I have shown a general plan, and various alternative arrangements.

A tunnel is almost essential if a railway is to have its self-respect, and this means a lot of trouble keeping the inside clear of dirt, leaves and small livestock. I have sketched a suggested arrangement which allows some of the accumulated debris to fall out of harm's way, although it cannot solve the problem. Obviously then, a tunnel should have an access lid of some sort.

Buildings outdoors are quite a problem in rough weather, though I believe that any wooden structure, well painted with polyurethene paint, should be able to take quite a pounding and still keep a good old British stiff upper lip. Because of this, and because wood is the best medium for most people, I have sketched a few buildings in this material.

Lakes and rivers are a matter of taste, and will naturally need some maintenance. I feel that fountains would look a little out of place, but see nothing against a small waterfall, worked by one of the electric pumps sold for such purposes.

I have shown various other ideas, all of which are intended not so much as things to copy exactly but as feeders for ideas. Very carefully I have left the horticultural side of things to those better equipped to deal with them. Nevertheless, I do feel that these marvellously narrow gauge L.G.B. trains are more likely to enhance their leafy backgrounds than would anything on a smaller scale.

Head-on view of an L.G.B. 0–4–0 tank engine of the sort Alex Bowie has in mind.

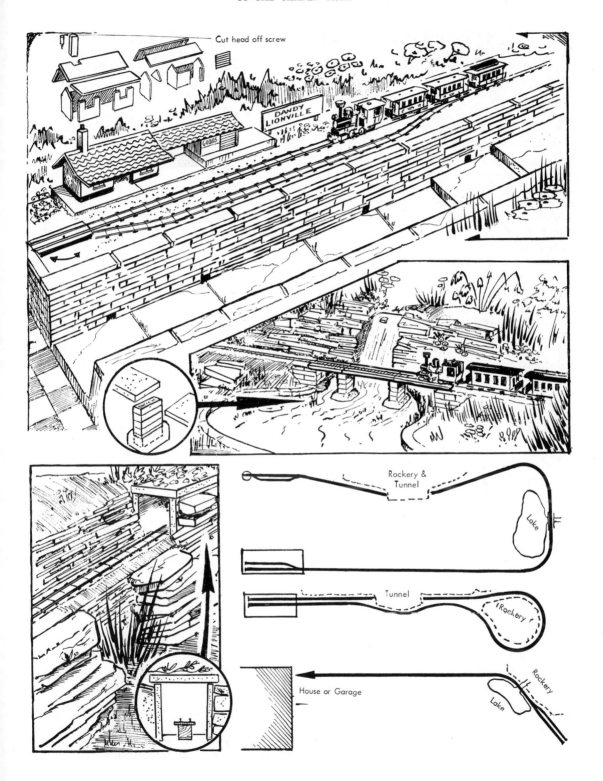

Cut head off screw

DANDY LIONVILLE

GOODS

Rockery & Tunnel

Lake

Tunnel

Rockery

House or Garage

Rockery

Lake

# Spectator at Shrewsbury

## by W. A. Tuplin

AT Shrewsbury one could never see a train going fast as one might at (say) Doncaster, but that was about the only railway enthusiast's delight that Shrewsbury lacked. On any summer Saturday in the 1930s the station was full of railway activity. Long distance trains stopped and re-started with or without change of engine London–Aberystwyth trains came in and reversed. Branch line trains came in, terminated and were re-arranged for going out again. Goods trains came through the station in one direction, and passed outside it in the other direction. A wide variety of locomotive classes of the LMS and GW systems regularly visited the station. What made the LMS contribution most notable was the regular 'running-in' practice of allotting newly-built and newly-repaired locomotives to stopping trains and others between Crewe and Shrewsbury.

The Great Western engine then came back tender-first towards the train as cautiously (it seemed) as if it were hidden from the driver by a thick fog, and the tender often creaked and groaned as if it were objecting to being pushed. If a mass of 120 tons were to strike the train even at walking pace it would shake passengers up quite markedly and so the driver had to be careful in backing-on and leaned well out of the cab to get the best view he could of the impending contact of the buffers. (When tenders were low he might get a good view of the end of the coach over the top of the coal). He might aim to stop with the buffers just touching and then open the regulators to 'ease up' for coupling. Alternatively he might aim to make the buffers strike at such a speed that an immediate full application of the brake would stop the engine and hold it with the buffer-spring fully compressed.

Between the buffers, the fireman first of all lifted a shackle onto its hook and tightened up the screw-coupling appropriately to what he could see to be the compression of the buffer springs. If they were fully compressed, hard tightening of the coupling might create very great difficulty and delay in detaching the engine at the end of its journey because it could not then compress the buffer springs from a standing start as tightly as it had done when hitting the train with little speed.

With the coupling 'on' the fireman then connected the vacuum brake pipes and called out 'Blow up' to tell the driver that he might start the ejector to create a vacuum in the train-pipe and brake cylinders. Then, if it were in the official heating season, he would connect up the heating pipes and open the cocks behind them. He would take the lamp from the back of the tender to the front of the engine and place it on a bracket near one end of the buffer beam so that in conjunction with the lamp already at the other side, the engine would be seen by railway staff to be heading an 'express passenger train or breakdown train proceeding to the scene of an accident'.

While at the front of the engine he might apply a jerking pull to the outer handle on the smokebox-door just to be sure that it was as tightly shut as he could make it.

Back on the footplate he would move a handle to blow steam for a moment through the boiler water-gauge and thus to make sure that no partial blockage of passages might be producing a false reading. He would take a look at the fire and perhaps add a few shovelfuls of coal to it. This was unusual, as Great Western practice of loading the back end of the firebox with coal nearly up to the top of the firehole almost guaranteed at this stage that there was no thin place in the fire.

The driver set the engine in fore-gear and checked that the ejector had produced 24 inches of vacuum. Usually the safety valve was by this time blowing slightly and so the men knew that the boiler pressure, whatever the gauge might show, was as high as it could possibly be. So they were ready to go as soon as the starting signal and the guard's flag gave them permission and authority to do so.

Then, regulator wide open for a moment got the train off the mark, but a quarter opening was enough for a slow slip-free start on the right hand bend that leads to the south. Only after a quarter of a mile was the engine made to pull hard to get up to Stretton. Then it's easy to Hereford and she might touch 'eighty' below Craven Arms.

Furthermore a Pacific that would take one of the night trains from Crewe to Glasgow or Perth might bring a train to Shrewsbury during the day-time as a 'filling-in' duty. So one might see at Shrewsbury the very latest development in LMS locomotive practice and at the same time some delightful old double-frame Great Western o-6-o or 4-4-o. All the Great Western 4-6-os were to be seen, with the exception of the 'Kings'. Engines of that class did appear via Pontypool Road in the 1950s but the experiment did not last long.

Shrewsbury station was so busy that it was impossible for any one person to see everything that went on. Perhaps the best single vantage-point was at the south-east corner of the island platform. Besides being good in itself, the site had the advantage of a foot-bridge giving access to all platforms. There was no view from the bridge or from any of the steps, as all were solidly covered with heavy timber and translucent glass in mid-Victorian style, but at least one could cross at any time without danger or annoyance to anyone.

The easternmost through platform received the 'North to West' main line trains from Liverpool and Manchester to Pontypool Rd, Severn Tunnel, Bristol and points west via Exeter. For such trains the south end of this platform was an engine-changing point and therefore specially useful to those spectators with intelligent interest in loco-motives and their work.

The 'North to West' trains were normally brought from Crewe to Shrewsbury by any of six classes of LMS 4-6-0 or, going far enough back in time, a Midland compound or North Western 'George the Fifth' 4-4-0. In the 1920s the engine might be a non-superheated 'Experi-ment' or 'Precursor'. The train always came in slowly, firstly because it had usually been stopped at the home signal, and secondly because entry to the east platform is by a sharp curve.

When the engine of a newly-arrived train was to be detached, the fireman dropped onto the platform and walked forward to take a lamp off the buffer beam so that its lamp-aspect no longer signified 'express train' and transferred the lamp to the back of the tender where it would indicate 'last vehicle'. Whilst the fireman was doing this the driver would be setting the engine from 'fore-gear' to 'back-gear' and on some LMS engines this could be quite a struggle because of

Royal Scot 4-6-0-6126 'Sanspareil' as originally built. Later it became 'Royal Army Service Corps'. Photo by London Midland Region (B.R.).

tightness of valve-rings in steam-chest liners. All piston-valves in Great Western engines had steam-expanded piston-rings and with no steam in the steam-chests, hand-reversing was easy.

The fireman slipped down between the platform-edge and the buffers behind the tender and his first job was to uncouple the vacuum brake pipes by lifting them at the joint and giving them opposite twists so as to disengage the horns. He would place the pipe on the tender or its 'dummy' so that its end was sealed. If steam heating was in use, he would turn off both cocks and separate the pipes at the joint.

The next job was to slacken the screw-coupling between the engine and tender so that the 'loose' end of it could be lifted off the hook. A strong man might unscrew the coupling in spite of the friction caused by the tension in it but he would find it slow and laborious. Instead the fireman shouted 'Ease-up' as a signal to the driver to open the regulator so as to cause the engine to move backwards, compressing the buffer-springs and moving the tender coupling-hook so close to that on the coach that the coupling became slack enough to allow the fireman to lift the

shackle clear of the hook and then to let it drop. This was not so easy as it looked to an observer on the platform as the standard coupling weighs about half a hundredweight.

In 'easing-up', even though it meant a movement of only a few inches, the engine and tender gained some momentum and this enabled them to compress the buffer springs more than the same piston-pressure could do with everything at rest. At the end of the first easing-up movement the coupling was at its slackest and an alert fireman would get the shackle off the hook at that moment, before the tender was moved away from the train by the buffer springs. If he missed the critical instant, he might find that he could not get the shackle off later without unscrewing the coupling. It was interesting to note what difficulties even an alert fireman might meet in this unobtrusive operation of 'hooking off'.

The fireman made his way back to the footplate either along the station platform on one side of the tender or along the permanent way on the other. As soon as the driver saw his mate returning, he would release the brakes and wind the engine into fore gear. As he entered the cab the fireman would say 'Away' if the starting-signal was 'off' or "When you can get" if it was 'on' and in the latter case the driver would sound the whistle to let the signalman know that they hadn't got

'King' Class 4–6–0 heading North. No. 6018 'King Henry VI' on an excursion from Paddington to Wolverhampton, approaching Widney Manor station. 15/3/59.
*Photo by Michael Mensing.*

'Hall' class 4924 'Eydon Hall' approaching Rugby (G.C.) with the 11.16 a.m. Bournemouth to York train. 26/5/58.
*Photo by Michael Mensing.*

all day to play about in. When the signal cleared, the driver would move the engine smartly out of the station, along a line curving left towards Wellington, till it was out of sight behind rows of coaches 'parked' on curved sidings.

As soon as the departing engine had moved clear, the signalman set the points and pulled a signal off for the relieving engine to move forward from its position outside the station onto the Wellington line before backing onto the train. The engine might be a 'Castle', 'Star', 'Saint', 'Hall' or 'Grange' and if this was to be its first run of the day it would be 'cold' and sluggish. Because the cylinders were cold and thus liable to turn steam into a dangerous quantity of water, the cylinder-cocks would be left open and the engine would creep along, softly puffing in a low cloud of hissing steam. This movement usually looked very leisurely compared with what was often a lively succession of snappy actions in getting the LMS engine off its train. It seemed as if the enginemen were far less anxious to get onto the job that to get off it, but this was largely illusion.

Nameplate of modified "Merchant Navy" Class Locomotive No. 35015 "Rotterdam Lloyd".
*Photo by Museum of British Transport, Clapham.*

# South Wales

## by Norman E. Preedy

WHERE better to begin an introduction on South Wales than Newport in 1964? Our train the 8.50 am Paddington to Swansea, 'The South Wales Pullman' has just halted in the spacious platforms of Newport's High Street Station. Head end power of our train is Castle class locomotive 5077 'Fairey Battle' of Swansea's Llandore Depot, and only weeks outshopped from Swindon with its immaculate new coat of green livery and copper and brass shining in the warm sun. At Newport begins the speciality of South Wales the Collet 56XX 0–6–2 tank engines, which with the 42XX 2–8–0s handle much of the coal trains. A vast array of lines, Eastern valleys and Western valleys come tumbling down from the coalfield into the docks of Newport and Cardiff, and Newport seems to belong more to Wales than to England, though it is in that curious frontier county, Monmouthshire.

The guard's flag shows green from the far end of the platform and with a shrill whistle from 'Fairey Battle' the brakes are eased off and the regulator is opened. The true staccato music of the Great Western echoes back as the 5077 moves away without a slip and heads into the 742 yds long High Street tunnel.

Barely 12 miles separate Newport from Cardiff but in that short distance there is much of interest to be seen, we are now heading out into the daylight after Newport tunnel, lines diverge rightward down which there flowed before 1923 L.N.W. trains from the Sirhowey Valley, Brecon and Merthyr traffic from the Rhymney Valley and beyond, coal trains of the Alexandra Dock and Railway Company, as well as heavy traffic from Ebbw Vale.

Newport boasts two Locomotive Depots, the largest is seen on the right and is called the 86A EBBW JUNCTION, this depot houses the big freight tanks and also the B.R. 9F 2–10–0s not to mention Halls, Granges, 28XX, 38XX, and the smaller 0–6–0. P.T.s. The other Newport Depot is Pill coded 86B this is located in the dockland and its allocation comprises of tank engines only for work in and around the docks, which occupy the neck of land between the Usk and Ebbw rivers, with another of Newport's landmarks the

Collet 0–6–0 2225 halts at Grange Court Station with an afternoon Hereford to Gloucester train, 1959.
*Photo By N. E. Preedy.*

Collet 0–6–2T 6649 at Aberdare 1958.
*Photo by N. E. Preedy.*

famous Transporter Bridge towering above them.

From the outskirts of Newport to Cardiff the railway strikes an almost dead level path through rather featureless landscape, which in no way taxes the output of our motive power, and with a glimpse of the broad Severn Estuary beyond St. Mellons we cross the Rhymney river and enter Cardiff, Wales' largest city and county town of Glamorgan.

Cardiff Dockland was once the busiest coal-exporting port in the world and can be seen sprawling away from the approaches to the station. With the South Wales coal boom came the independent railways to encourage this growth of dockland.

After the opening of the Taff Vale railway from Merthyr in 1841 (later it topped the Aberdare, Rhondha and other valleys), the East Dock was added and following the arrival of the Rhymney Railway in 1858 the North Basin came into being.

The Rhymney Railway had its headquarters at Caerphilly on the outskirts of Cardiff and here approximately 500 men were employed at the locomotive works compared to the 15,000 at Swindon.

There was capacity for some sixty small engines in 'this Swindon of South Wales' that was overlooked except by those inside G.W.R. circles.

This was where the 56XX and 66XX locomotives of South Wales together with the pannier tanks came for their overhauls.

Cardiff was supplied with four locomotive depots including the dockland depot of 88B CARDIFF EAST DOCK, 88A CATHAYS with its large sub-shed at RADYR which, when CATHAYS closed took over the 88A code. To these depots in the main were allocated the freight locomotives and the tank locomotives for the local passenger work.

Once again the whistle of 5077 shrills and we are again given the treat of hearing that sure footed start without a slip as she sets course for Bridgend, crossing the maze of points and trackwork. Soon after leaving Cardiff General station we pass the largest and most well known of the Cardiff depots, this is CANTON coded 86C which houses the large passenger locomotives and whose fame for turning out a clean engine is second to none in the Region. Its top link Castles, Kings and Britannias are showpieces in engine cleanliness.

From Ely the railway begins a gradual ascent up the valley of the Ely river over $2\frac{1}{2}$ miles at 1 in 106 to 187, before the summit is reached just east of Llanharan. Apart from the pits and tips which are scattered over the landscape, (Llanharan is an isolated outpost of the southern outcrop of the coalfield) the fertile plain of south Glamorgan is still unspoilt and given over to agriculture.

At Bridgend we halt for two minutes from 12.16 to 12.18, once away from Bridgend (which

2–8–2T 7205 at Radyr MPD. Cardiff. 1/6/63.
*Photo by N. E. Preedy.*

was approached from both directions on curves over which a 40 m.p.h. speed restriction was imposed), we are at Pyle a few miles on from Bridgend. Margam is the next point of interest with all its heavy steel industry which dominates the skyline. Also to be seen is the modern Abbey works of the Steel Company of Wales which was opened in 1951.

Beyond the steel works of Margam, the docks of Port Talbot on the estuary of the Afon river come into view on the left. We halt at Port Talbot for three minutes from 12.36 to 12.39. Any locomotives seen are likely to come from DUF-FRYN YARD depot coded 87B which serves the area. The next stop for the South Wales Pullman and our penultimate one is Neath whose locomotive depot at COURT START coded 87A is passed before entering the station again approached over restricted 40 m.p.h. curves. The Neath stop is from 12.49 to 12.51 and after leaving there is a climb at 1 in 99 to 88 for two miles to a summit just beyond Skewen. After this the line drops down to 1 in 191 to 106 through Llansamlet and again after a short up hill section down a very steep bank from LLANDORE, the home of 'Fairy Battle' and Swansea's principal locomotive depot and in to Swansea's terminal High Street station where arrival is "on time" at 1.10.

Apart from LLANDORE coded 87E which is home to the large passenger locomotives, the Castles, and Counties, the Halls and the Granges, Swansea is provided with three other depots which cater for the freight locomotives which work into the area.

These depots are SWANSEA EAST DOCK 87D which is next in size to LLANDORE and boasted various large and small tank locomotives, together with the odd Hall or 2–8–0 which worked into the area. The other main depot was DANYGRAIG coded 87C. At this depot, which was quite an impressive brick building were allocated the small Swansea Harbour Trust 0–4–0 tank locomotives and the Powesland and Mason locomotives of Peckitt design, these little locomotives could be seen working in the streets and on the Dockside. A Sunday morning visit to the depot at DANYGRAIG could be relied upon to secure for the photographer some worthwhile photographs of these superb little engines.

In addition to these depots, there was also a small one at Swansea Victoria and this was coded 87K.

South Wales being so concerned with heavy steel industry it came as no surprise that with the end of steam power on British Railways that various contractors would see a use for the copper, brass and steel to be found in a locomotive and with this many scrapyards sprung up in the area.

Perhaps the most notorious of them all is that of Woodham Bros. at Barry where even at the present time some 200 locomotives lie rusting away. Amongst these one time proud workhorses lie such famous names as Duke of Gloucester, Defiant (even in death), Manston, Port Line and King Edward I to mention a few. In addition lie many other of the lesser known types, but classes which worked the life line of goods trains and were never accredited with the limelight of their larger brothers. 2–8–0s of the Western Region and G.W.R. design stand with the modern Standard Heavy goods loco the 9F 2–10–0 and also the little tank locomotives of the 2–6–2 wheel arrangement which covered the Devon and Cornish branch lines.

Perhaps the other largest yards are at Cashmores and United Wagon Works at Newport and it was at the former where I saw one of my favourite Bulleid Pacifics 34006 Bude (the one time pride of Salisbury Depot) reduced to a heap of unrecognisable steel in a matter of hours.

I will end this article on a happy note. Preservation Societies have sprung up whilst engines have been standing at Barry and attention has turned to these with the happy result that already an ex Somerset and Dorset 2–8–0 and Manor class

4–6–0 7827 have been saved. Proceedings are also under way for a 45XX 2–6–2T and a Midland 4F 0–6–0 is already safe and sound ready to run on the K.W.V.R. line in Yorkshire. No doubt there will be others.

So whilst taking a walk through the silent lines of engines at Barry, whose fires have long since been extinguished and whose smell of warm oil and steam has gone, one can rest assured that although B.R. steam finished on 11th August 1968 it still lives on in the shape of the many preserved lines up and down the country and for this we must be thankful.

In closing I will say that I have enjoyed every moment of the time spent with my camera on the lineside (yes even the wet days on Shap trudging through the waist-high grass) and have made a host of friends both among the Railway Staff and elsewhere.

View of Aberbeeg looking towards Newport, with 52XX and 62XX in view. 1959. *Photo by N. E. Preedy.*

*Top:*     'West Country' class Pacific 34038 'Lynton' arriving at Bournemouth Central with the 5.10 p.m. departure for Waterloo. 3/7/64.
*Photo by Douglas Doherty.*

*Bottom:*     Imminent for departure from Waterloo is re-built 'Merchant Navy' 35017 35017 'Belgian Marine'.
*Photo by Keith Pirt.*

Diesel-Electric locomotive No. 10201
on down local out of Euston passing
Camden MPD.
*Photo by Douglas Doherty.*

The prototype English Electric 'Deltic'
locomotive backing out of the
platform at King's Cross.
*Photo by Douglas Doherty.*

A Western Region cross country DMU
arrives at Salisbury with the 12.35
Cardiff-Portsmouth train on 12th April
1968.
*Photo by G. F. Gillham.*

# How I made my Model Engine

## by Edward Bowness

I am working in a clothier's shop starting at half past eight o'clock in the morning and finishing at eight o'clock at night. I have an hour at noon for dinner and half an hour at four o'clock for tea. We close at noon on Wednesdays, but on Saturdays we keep open till half past ten.

This winter I am attending the Geometrical Drawing class, and last winter I passed second class in Drawing in Light and Shade. My ambition is to become a locomotive engineer, if I can obtain a situation.

In the summer of 1896 I got Mr. Clement Stretton's book on the Development of the Locomotive. I particularly liked the Midland Railway 7ft. 6in. single bogie locomotive, No. 1853, illustrated there, and when I found out that the general colour of the Midland Railway locomotives is dark red, I decided to make a model of that locomotive. I made it to the scale of $\frac{3}{16}$ in. to the foot.

I started the plans for the locomotive on August 3rd, 1897, and finished them on October 22nd, 1897. I started making the engine on October 25th, 1897, and finished making it on January 28th, 1898. I made the tender in about two weeks, starting it on February 1st, 1898, and finishing it on February 15th, 1898. I had to hurry with the making of the tender as I did not hear of the competition until January 31st, 1898. First of all I made them out of one piece of card. Since I designed the locomotive I have found out that the frames are made first and the footplates fastened around them afterwards, but I did not know

this then. The engine has double frames, the sides of the firebox beneath the footplates being cut in one piece with the frames. The top edge of the front of the firebox is curved so that the boiler can rest on it. The cylinders are made out of two pieces of pencil cut to the required length with the lead pushed out. There are no pistons, the piston rod merely sliding through the space where the lead formerly was. One end of each piston rod is hammered out flat so that it can fit in the fork in the connecting rod. I first intended making a built up crank axle, but I found it impossible in so small a size. I finally made a bent wire crank axle. In order to get it in its place I had to cut triangular pieces of card out of the four frames. When the connecting rods were put on, and the axle fitted, the same pieces of card which were cut out were put back again and glued in their places. The bogie frames are fastened together by a broad piece of card. This is fastened to another piece of card of the same size. The top piece is fastened to the frames. The pivot by which the bogie is fastened on the engine is made of two eyelets one pushed inside the other. The eyelets are used for putting in the laceholes of shoes and as my father is a shoemaker, I could easily get these. Two curved pieces of card are glued on to the bogie. The top surface of each of these pieces of card is blackleaded and the corresponding parts on the top piece are also blackleaded so they slide very easily. The wheels are cut out of a double thickness of very hard card. The flanges and outside rims of the wheels

94

are rings of thin card glued on afterwards. The centres of the wheels are circles of card glued on, one inside and one outside. The bogie wheels have two circles of card outside, the outer ones covering the ends of the axles as they have not outside bearings. The feed pipes and the brake pipes are pieces of wire, cut to the required length and bent into shape. I wound strips of paper around the ends of these wires one half being on the wire and the other half projecting and forming a tube, so that the wires on the tender can be fitted into them. The springs are pieces

of card glued on to the frames. They have no connection with the axleboxes. Each axlebox is formed of two pieces of card. The larger one has a hole in it for the end of the axle to fit in. The smaller piece of card has no hole in it as it covers the end of the axle.

There is a strip of card at the back end of the support for the smokebox. It does not go quite down to the footplates but just leaves room for the guide to go under. The front of the smokebox was next put up. A strip of thin card was then bent over it, this forming the cover of the smoke-

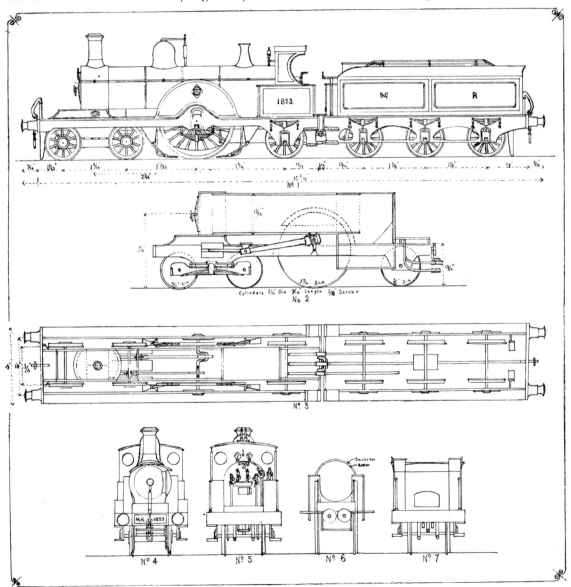

box. The boiler is made of paper wound around a stick of the required diameter. The end that was to go in the firebox is not as thick as the other parts of the tube there not being as many thicknesses of paper wound around it. As the paper was wound around the stick it was glued so it made a very good tube. When it was quite dry I made a cut in each side in the shape of an arc. The parts so loosened I pressed in so that the sides of the boiler did not rub against the driving wheels. I may here mention that drawing No. 6 is not a section, but just a drawing showing the position of the cylinders. It also shows how far the sides of the boiler were pressed in, and explains more fully what I have been saying. The end of the firebox was next put on, and pieces of card the shape of a right-angled triangle were put in front to keep it upright. The firebox casing is a piece of card bent over the boiler and the end of the firebox, the front corners of it being cut away to fit the splashers. The thickness of the card made the thinner part of the tube as thick, on the top, as the other part. The cab was next made. The windows are made of a very transparent substance, often used for wrapping sweets in. The reversing screw is made of an ordinary screw, with a piece of wire bent into the required shape, glued in the notch in the head of the screw. The regulator is made of a piece of wire, bent into shape, and glued on to the upper part of the firebox casing. The two pressure-gauges are just pieces of card, glued on to the front of the cab in their proper places. In the centre of the back of the firebox casing there is a small shelf. The injectors, brake apparatus, water gauges, and furnace door, are just painted being of too small a scale to model them. The funnel, dome, and steam-funnel are made of wood. The top of the funnel is made the proper shape, by a ring of card being glued around it about 1/24 in. from the top. On the top of the dome a small circle of card was glued and on this the levers for the safety-valves are fastened. The springs are represented by strips of paper wound around the wires. The steam funnel is not painted but just glued, on the white wood. This gives it the appearance of polished brass. The whistle is made of a pin with the head left on. A strip of paper was wound around it. A piece of wire is connected to the whistle from the cab, the end in the cab being turned up to represent the handle. Each buffer is made of an eyelet with a rivet pushed in. I got the rivet out of my father's shop. The

hook is made of a pin with the head cut off and just a small piece cut off the point. It is bent to the proper shape, and pushed in a hole in the centre of the buffer-beam. The flexible brake coupling is made of a piece of string. A pin is pushed up the string and the top of it bent downwards, to hold the string in its proper position. Two small pieces of card are glued partly on the end of the string, and two corresponding pieces on the string on the vehicle to be attached to it, would fit in the spaces and complete a small circle of card. I found this out myself, never having seen it in use before. The footplate on the tender is just a rectangle of card. There are just two frames. The wheels, axleboxes, and springs, are made the same way as those on the engine. In the centre of the tender beneath the footplates, I glued a piece of pencil with the lead pushed out, to represent the vacuum brake cylinder. A piece of wire runs through the cylinder, and is connected to the brake pipe on the engine. The line clearers are not bent but are directly behind the wheels. A small square of card is placed between the frames and the line clearers and this strengthens them considerably. The coping on the tender is made by bending outwards the upper edges on the sides. The rails along the top of the tender are kept parallel by pieces of cotton. I put small pieces of coal in the tender. As I put it in I poured thin glue over it so none of it dropped out when I held it upside down next morning.

I used three colours of paint, viz:- light red, dark red and black. The paint is mixed with liquid gum so it has a glossy appearance. The general colour of the locomotive is dark red. I have painted a mark of light red about $\frac{1}{16}$ in. wide around some of the parts. On each side of this is a fine black mark. For the marks around the boiler I painted three thin narrow strips of paper light red with a fine black line down the centre. The tender is painted the same colours as the engine. The blurred appearance of the photograph was caused by the paint not lying as well on the glued surfaces as on the card.

*This article—by a 14-year old boy—first appeared in a* **Model Engineer** *about the turn of the century and is inserted without alteration. The boy in question achieved his ambition of working with models and enjoyed a lifetime of boat modelling, as Editor of* **Ships & Ship Models** *and as marine editor of* **Model Engineer.** *We do not know if he still cherished his first love for locomotives!*

# Lineside Huts

## by J. L. Flann

LINESIDE huts form one of those simple features which add so much to the realism of any layout. Look at the prototype, and here and there you will see different huts fulfilling many different functions, but which can be modelled with the minimum of effort. All you need is a piece of good quality mounting card, various building papers, perhaps some 'corrugated iron' and the odd pot of paint. Modellers will have most of these materials to hand already. Windows, to my mind, make or marr the appearance of any model building and, for a choice, invest in an Airfix station building kit and there you will find a really good selection of windows which suit this kind of building.

The sketch shows the essential dimensions. These do not, of course, have to be followed rigidly, provided that the basic proportions are not upset. Commence construction by cutting out the two sides and two ends. Then, in one end, cut out the opening for the door and, in one side, the window opening. The exact size of the latter is determined by the Airfix window which you are going to use. The point is, however, that these windows (for this purpose) look better if they are put in from the inside sideways and 'inside out', so the size of the opening is determined accordingly. The other thing to note is that if you want a 'timber' hut, the card should be scribed vertically at $\frac{1}{8}$ in. intervals before the pieces are cut out.

Assembly is straightforward, with sides fitting inside the ends. If it is to be a brick or stone hut, the brick paper should be put in place before the door and window are positioned. If it is to be timber, and most huts of this sort were, put the window in place and, for the door, insert behind the opening a vertically scribed piece of card, but leave a gap at the bottom for the card doorstep. Over the door opening, put a lintel of postcard and, below the window, a sill from the same material. The roof can then be measured and cut from one piece of card. Bend it along the ridge line from a cut nearly through the material, and stick in place, remembering to allow for the chimney. Most of these huts sport a chimney piece, but some do not. This can be a simple piece of tube to simulate a stove pipe, or more elaborate as shown in the drawing.

The beauty of these little huts is that no matter how many you make, they can all be different— some finished as 'timber', either natural brown or painted, some covered with brick or stone papers. The roofs can either be covered with slate paper or scored to imitate felt and painted black, or covered with 'corrugated iron' and painted black, brown or grey. The change can be rung with chimneys and windows as well, without departing from the basic hut

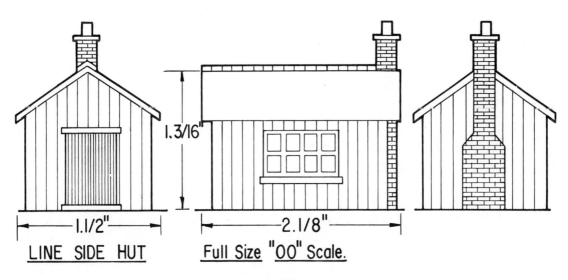

1.3/16"

|— 1.1/2" —|
LINE SIDE HUT    Full Size "OO" Scale.

— 2.1/8" —

97

# Building a Regency House

## *An attractive 4 mm. scale structure* by Maurice Kelly

THE steam locomotive is not the only thing which is fast disappearing from sight nowadays. In recent years there has been a regrettable increase in the number of demolitions of houses of this type in the town where I live. So often is it the case that a house which has stood for more than 120 years, and is in addition one of the original houses of the town, has disappeared, to be replaced by another block of human rabbit hutches, that I decided some time ago to make a record of such buildings before it was too late. This is in keeping with the whole occupation of railway modelling, for I suspect that many committed modellers purposely select items for modelling which are likely to disappear in the next few years. I know also that many models are made of prototypes which have long since ceased to exist, and so we are helping to preserve an accurate picture of the fine things which our children will never see. Whenever possible, I have taken measurements and photographs of the best of local architecture, and I had my eye on

the subject of this article for some months. When, after a change of ownership, it was completely repainted outside, I felt that this was the moment.

This was, in its time, a fairly large town house. The façade is well proportioned, the columned porch giving a dignified focal point. It is difficult to imagine when the lean-to on the corner was added, and the detailing in the form of pilasters on the small piece of wall is also rather curious. This house might have had a stable when new, but there is now no sign of one. The owners probably used a livery stable, and there are remnants of such establishments in the district. All told, I felt it worthy of a model, although as usual this took much longer than anticipated, as I became rather engrossed with the garden. In the original, this is in a sorry state, and usually holds several taxis and a motor coach. The house must be full of taxi drivers.

Construction was complicated by the fact that I wished to fit the model, as in the prototype, on to

GROUND LEVEL

0 1 2 3 4 5 6 7 8 9 10    15    20    25    30    35    40 FEET

Rear view of Maurice Kellys' Regency House clearly shows the rockery garden described in the text.

a falling site, and that at the front of the house there is a basement area. To start with, I cut a baseboard for the house, with 6 ft. or so extra on all sides, and including a slot for the basement area. This base was mounted on blocks until the shell of the house, complete with basement walls and floor, was in position. Then the whole was mounted on a box of 2 in. × 1 in. timber on edge, the side pieces being cut down roughly to form the falling ground level. The house was then finished, the garden walls erected, and the plaster/sawdust surface of the garden built up.

In the general construction of the house and garden, there are only a few things worth mentioning.

## RAILINGS

These were built up on a wooden jig. Copper wire was used, after stretching. One end was gripped in the vice and a steady pull given with a pair of pliers on the other. You can feel the wire extend, and this straightens and hardens it at the same time.

## BALCONY

Somewhere I had seen a suggested jig for this sort of job, consisting of a shallow tray into which fireclay was rolled to give a flat bed. Wire is cut and shaped and pressed into this mould to be held whilst soldering is done. Then a brush with soldering fluid and a touch of a gas flame, and the blobs of solder flow away, making a clean job. I made such a jig, but had scant success. It could be that my wire was too thin, but I had to resort to little pieces of clay to hold the ends of the wires down. The very small pieces certainly stayed put, but the blobs of solder did not run under the gas flame. All the same, a better job was done than if I had not used a jig at all. I shall persevere and find out what I have been doing wrong; the scheme certainly sounds feasible.

## ROCKERY AND FLOWER BEDS

It has always seemed to me a sensible idea, wherever possible to use the full-size material of its representation in the model. A small knob of anthracite, hit with a hammer, produces tons of model coal. This has only one disadvantage. Over the months, the coal goes white, due to some reaction. I found that if sufficient coal for the particular job were whisked up in a jar with the right amount of eggshell varnish, this varnish not only holds the coal together and fixes it in position, but also prevents the whitening process. So it was that, when I wanted to build a rockery, I reduced a small piece of rockery stone from the surrounds of my garden railway to suitably sized pieces with a hammer and, finally with a pair of pliers. These pieces were then stuck in position with UHU and a pair of tweezers. For earth in the flower beds, I used sieved dried earth, which looks, not surprisingly, just right. Bedding plants were made by dropping small blobs of Evostik Resin-W one-way wet adhesive in the correct positions and sprinkling with dried sawdust. When set, and the surplus brushed off, a few touches with a brush loaded with pure poster colour produced an excellent simulation of various coloured flowers. Rows of vegetables were glue plus sawdust alone. One greenhouse is empty, but the other contains pot plants and seedlings in boxes. The seed boxes are rectangles of thick card coated with glue and earth, and finally spotted with paint. For me, the main advantage of 4 mm. scale is that one can indulge in such small details without too much difficulty. In a larger scale I imagine that one would not find it so easy. Is this the reason why so few, if any, of pre-war model railways were as completely modelled as the majority are today?

Random Thoughts (*cont. from opposite page*)
age by many years. Peter Warlock, composer of *The Capriole Suite*, contributed articles on South Welsh railways to the *Railway Magazine* under his real name of Philip Heseltine. Honnegger's descriptive music *Pacific 231* is too well known for us to be in any doubts as to this composer's interests! Many churches and cathedrals hide railway enthusiasts behind their organ consoles—indeed, the ties between the organ and railways seem incredibly close, and of course,

combine trains, church and music in a unique way. I personally know of eight such railway-minded organists, none of whom can explain the alchemy which led them on these parallel paths. Followers of Freud have told us that the organ console, with its stops and controls and great unleashings of power, is a mental substitute for a locomotive footplate—a fairly dubious argument I feel. It would be a sight easier to become an engineman and have the real thing (well no, perhaps nowadays it wouldn't).

# Random Thoughts on Railway Enthusiasts

## by John Brewer

RACING has been called the 'Sport of Kings', but railways as a hobby have always attracted a large following of, if not exactly kings, certainly of famous persons. The early years of railways in this country, curiously, saw little support from the intelligentsia. Most famous of the anti-railway brigade was John Ruskin, art critic, writer, naturalist, artist and exponent of the Gothic Revival. Ruskin was most things, but he was emphatically *not* a railway enthusiast. The building of the Midland Railway through the Lake District filled him with such fury that he wrote some of the best anti-railway articles ever penned. Looking back from the safe distance of over a century, he sounds irritable and pedantic, but he was only expressing exactly the same point of view as has been aired since against, successively, the encroachment of electricity pylons, airports and motorways into the rural landscape. He detested the raw scars of new railway lines cut into the green hills, and the idea of railway preservation as we know it today would have been anathema and absurd to him. Just imagine, in a distant 21st century, an appeal to preserve the M1 and the motor cars which run on it!

Like most kicking out against the tide of change and progress, Ruskin's vitriolic writings had very little effect, and rail travel grew apace. The raw clay cuttings and masonry grew grass and weathered, and the railways blended into the 'traditional' British scene as manor houses, windmills and canals had done before them. Railways soon became invested with a fascination and romance which has never left them. Frith engraved Paddington Station, and Turner saw, in his painting *Rain, Steam and Speed*, the same sort of romance in Hanwell Viaduct as he saw in stormy seascapes. When the Great Western Railway ran its last broad gauge train in 1892, Horatio Brown was inspired to write a panegyric in verse of the best heroic kind. We had come a long way since John Ruskin and the Midland Railway.

Writers and poets began to draw heavily on railways as the subject for inspiration. Even Charles Dickens did, and his railway experiences were not of the happiest kind. It is almost impossible to believe that Trollope was not a railway enthusiast, and Hardy came dangerously close to a liking for traction engines. Since those days Siegfried Sassoon, Stephen Spender and W. H. Auden have written railway verse, and Sir John Betjeman's railway poems reveal a true enthusiast.

The attraction which railways have as a hobby for churchmen and musicians is also well known. Cynics have said that plenty of spare time and huge parsonages are the twin explanations of the railway modelling parson, but I do not believe this. Vicars known to me are very busy people and, in any case, there are plenty of alternative pursuits one can follow, given time and space, apart from model railways. I think we will find the answer more readily by examining the interest rather than its followers. Railways are essentially peaceful objects, and civilised, or rather *civilising*. When railways have been used for warlike purposes, it has always been in a rather indirect manner, with the possible exception of the American Civil War. Locomotives do not bristle with guns as do many otherwise attractive aircraft and ships. An intelligent interest in railways also encompasses an extraordinary wide range of 'fringe appeals' like topography, social history and architecture.

The appeal of railways to musicians is no less easy to explain. Some say that it has to do with the 'rhythm of the rail-joints' but I have always found this theory unconvincing. The great Czech composer Antonin Dvorak used to haunt Paddington Station and, it is said, send a messenger to report on the engines therein whenever he was not able to attend himself. The fact that some of his music has a railway 'sound' should not concern us too much—after all, so has some of Bach's, and that gentleman missed the railway

*(cont. on facing page)*

Leaving Doncaster heading homewards to March is B.17 61619 'Welbeck Abbey' with a stopping train.
*Photo by Douglas Doherty*

'County' class 4–6–0 1017 'County of Hereford' climbing past the site of Rhosrobin Halt, Wrexham on the 2.35p.m. Birkenhead—Paddington. 18/4/60.
*Photo by Michael Mensing*

Ivatt 4MT 2–6–0 43019 on 3.15 p.m. Swedish Lloyd line boat train to Tilbury waiting to leave St. Pancras. 21st October 1961.
*Photo by Michael Mensing*

B.R. class 8P 4–6–2 46202 'Princess Anne', re-built from turbine locomotive LMS 6202. The train is the 8.00 Euston–Liverpool, August 1952.
*Photo by London Midland Region* (*B.R.*)

Down West Country express running into Exeter Central behind Bulleid Pacific number 34003 'Plymouth'.
*Photo by Douglas Doherty*

Stopping train to Bletchley leaving Cambridge behind class 4 75036.
*Photo by Douglas Doherty*

Coming off the Blackpool coast line at Kirkham North Junction is a train for Manchester hauled by a Stanier 'Black Five' and piloted by 'Jubilee' 45710 'Irresistible'. The lines straight ahead into the distance lead to Blackpool North. The line coming down on the left is from Blackpool Central via the 'direct' line.
*Photo by Douglas Doherty*

46115 'Scots Guardsman' with a Euston to Blackpool relief leaving Rugby. 30/8/58.
*Photo by Douglas Doherty*

'Hall' class 4993 'Dalton Hall' hauling the 4.05 p,m. Wolverhampton (L.L.)—Oxford, near Widney Manor. 26/4/59.
*Photo by Michael Mensing.*

61664 'Liverpool' heading out of March towards Peterborough.
*Photo by Douglas Doherty.*

Moving empty stock out of Euston is Fowler 4MT 2–6–4T 42360. Camden MPD on right.
*Photo by Douglas Doherty.*

60157 'Great Eastern' leaving the carriage sidings at Doncaster.
*Photo by Douglas Doherty.*

The L.N.E.R. embarked upon a re-numbering scheme for its locomotives and 4472 became number 103. Upon Nationalisation in 1948, all L.N.E.R. locomotives had 60,000 added to their numbers, hence the number 60103 on 'Flying Scotsman's' cabside.
Here she accelerates away from Doncaster with a Leeds to London express in June 1961.
*Photo by Douglas Doherty.*

Down 'Golden Arrow' express about to leave Victoria behind 70004 'William Shakespeare'.
*Photo by Keith Pirt.*

46153 'The Royal Dragoon' heading the up 'The Mancunian' out of Rugby.
*Photo by Douglas Doherty.*

Other Gresley types, 2. The V2 class 'Green Arrows' were mixed traffic locomotives first appearing in 1936. The boilers were similar to 4472s but mounted on a 2–6–2 wheeled chassis.

In service they were equally at home on express passenger trains as on express freights. The pioneer V2 was named 'Green Arrow' as is seen here at Doncaster heading an up express freight train in British Railways days in August 1960.
*Photo by Douglas Doherty.*

# The Name on the Side

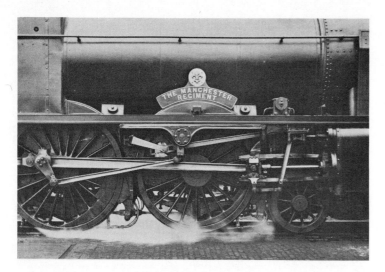

Close-up of L.M.S. Royal Scot 4–6–0 'The Manchester Regiment'.
*Photo by W. Potter.*

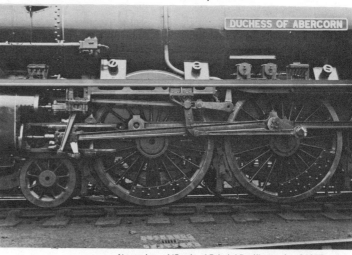

Close-up of Stanier 4–6–2 'Duchess of Abercorn', Crewe North MPD, August 1938.
*Photo by W. Potter.*

Close-up of nameplate of 'Lord Nelson' class engine number 30851.
*Photo by Douglas Doherty.*

Nameplate of 'Battle of Britain' Pacific number 34087.
*Photo by Museum of British Transport, Clapham.*

Nameplate of GWR 'Castle' 4079
*Photo by Keith Pirt.*

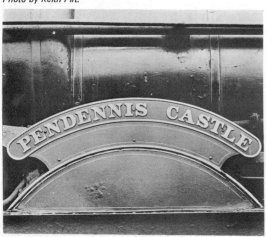

Nameplate of modified 'West Country' class locomotive 34012 'Launceston'.
Photo by Museum of British Transport, Clapham.

Nameplate of 'Merchant Navy' Pacific number 35019.
Photo by Museum of British Transport, Clapham.

Nameplate of 'Merchant Navy' Pacific number 35012.
Photo by Museum of British Transport, Clapham.

Nameplate of 'Merchant Navy' Pacific number 35005.
Photo by Museum of British Transport, Clapham.

Nameplate of 'Merchant Navy' Pacific number 35004.
Photo by Museum of British Transport, Clapham.

Close-up of the cab-side of 60106 'Flying Fox'. Photo by K. Pirt.

Close-up of nameplate of A4 number 60009. *Photo by Keith Pirt.*

'Battle of Britain' Pacific 34054 'Lord Beaverbrook' at Exmouth Junction MPD. *Photo by Douglas Doherty.*

Nameplate of 'West Country' class locomotive 210109 'Lyme Regis'. *Photo by Museum of British Transport, Clapham.*

Close-up of RH side of Gresley Pacific 'Flying Fox'. York MPD, 1953 *Photo by W. Potter.*

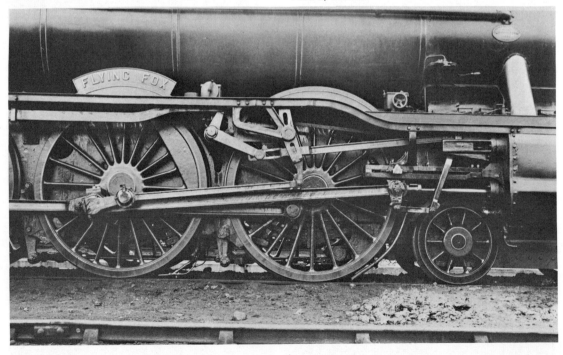